CW00350531

IELTS
GENERAL TRAINING 16

WITH ANSWERS

AUTHENTIC PRACTICE TESTS

9 1972 |

18 - oft 14

Cambridge University Press
www.cambridge.org/elt

Cambridge Assessment English
www.cambridgeenglish.org

Information on this title: www.cambridge.org/9781108933865

First published 2021

20 19 18 17 16 15 14 13 12 11 10 9 8 7 6 5 4 3 2 1

Printed in Dubai by Oriental Press

A catalogue record for this publication is available from the British Library

ISBN 978-1-108-93385-8 Academic Student's Book with Answers with Audio
ISBN 978-1-108-93386-5 General Training Student's Book with Answers with Audio

Contents

Introduction

Prepare for the exam with practice tests from Cambridge

Inside you'll find four authentic examination papers from Cambridge Assessment English. They are the perfect way to practise – EXACTLY like the real exam.

Why are they unique?

All our authentic practice tests go through the same design process as the IELTS test. We check every single part of our practice tests with real students under exam conditions, to make sure we give you the most authentic experience possible.

   Students can practise these tests on their own or with the help of a teacher to familiarise themselves with the exam format, understand the scoring system and practise exam technique.

Further information

IELTS is jointly managed by the British Council, IDP: IELTS Australia and Cambridge Assessment English. Further information can be found on the IELTS official website at ielts.org.

WHAT IS THE TEST FORMAT?

IELTS consists of four components. All candidates take the same Listening and Speaking tests. There is a choice of Reading and Writing tests according to whether a candidate is taking the Academic or General Training module.

Academic	General Training
For candidates wishing to study at undergraduate or postgraduate levels, and for those seeking professional registration.	For candidates wishing to migrate to an English-speaking country (Australia, Canada, New Zealand, UK), and for those wishing to train or study below degree level.

The test components are taken in the following order:

Listening 4 parts, 40 items, approximately 30 minutes		
Academic Reading 3 sections, 40 items 60 minutes	or	**General Training Reading** 3 sections, 40 items 60 minutes
Academic Writing 2 tasks 60 minutes	or	**General Training Writing** 2 tasks 60 minutes
Speaking 11 to 14 minutes		
Total Test Time 2 hours 44 minutes		

GENERAL TRAINING TEST FORMAT

Listening

This test consists of four parts, each with ten questions. The first two parts are concerned with social needs. The first part is a conversation between two speakers and the second part is a monologue. The final two parts are concerned with situations related to educational or training contexts. The third part is a conversation between up to four people and the fourth part is a monologue.

A variety of question types is used, including: multiple choice, matching, plan/map/ diagram labelling, form completion, note completion, table completion, flow-chart completion, summary completion, sentence completion and short-answer questions.

Candidates hear the recording once only and answer the questions as they listen. Ten minutes are allowed at the end for candidates to transfer their answers to the answer sheet.

Reading

This test consists of three sections with 40 questions. The texts are taken from notices, advertisements, leaflets, newspapers, instruction manuals, books and magazines. The first section contains texts relevant to basic linguistic survival in English, with tasks mainly concerned with providing factual information. The second section focuses on the work context and involves texts of more complex language. The third section involves reading more extended texts, with a more complex structure, but with the emphasis on descriptive and instructive rather than argumentative texts.

A variety of question types is used, including: multiple choice, identifying information (True/False/Not Given), identifying the writer's views/claims (Yes/No/Not Given), matching information, matching headings, matching features, matching sentence endings, sentence

5

completion, summary completion, note completion, table completion, flow-chart completion, diagram-label completion and short-answer questions.

Writing

This test consists of two tasks. It is suggested that candidates spend about 20 minutes on Task 1, which requires them to write at least 150 words, and 40 minutes on Task 2, which requires them to write at least 250 words. Task 2 contributes twice as much as Task 1 to the Writing score.

In Task 1, candidates are asked to respond to a given situation with a letter requesting information or explaining the situation. They are assessed on their ability to engage in personal correspondence, elicit and provide general factual information, express needs, wants, likes and dislikes, express opinions, complaints, etc.

In Task 2, candidates are presented with a point of view, argument or problem. They are assessed on their ability to provide general factual information, outline a problem and present a solution, present and justify an opinion, and to evaluate and challenge ideas, evidence or arguments.

Candidates are also assessed on their ability to write in an appropriate style. More information on assessing the Writing test, including Writing assessment criteria (public version), is available at ielts.org.

Speaking

This test takes between 11 and 14 minutes and is conducted by a trained examiner. There are three parts:

Part 1

The candidate and the examiner introduce themselves. Candidates then answer general questions about themselves, their home/family, their job/studies, their interests and a wide range of similar familiar topic areas. This part lasts between four and five minutes.

Part 2

The candidate is given a task card with prompts and is asked to talk on a particular topic. The candidate has one minute to prepare and they can make some notes if they wish, before speaking for between one and two minutes. The examiner then asks one or two questions on the same topic.

Part 3

The examiner and the candidate engage in a discussion of more abstract issues which are thematically linked to the topic in Part 2. The discussion lasts between four and five minutes.

The Speaking test assesses whether candidates can communicate effectively in English. The assessment takes into account Fluency and Coherence, Lexical Resource, Grammatical Range and Accuracy, and Pronunciation. More information on assessing the Speaking test, including Speaking assessment criteria (public version), is available at ielts.org.

HOW IS IELTS SCORED?

IELTS results are reported on a nine-band scale. In addition to the score for overall language ability, IELTS provides a score in the form of a profile for each of the four skills (Listening, Reading, Writing and Speaking). These scores are also reported on a nine-band scale. All scores are recorded on the Test Report Form along with details of the candidate's nationality, first language and date of birth. Each Overall Band Score corresponds to a descriptive statement which gives a summary of the English-language ability of a candidate classified at that level. The nine bands and their descriptive statements are as follows:

9 **Expert user** – *Has fully operational command of the language: appropriate, accurate and fluent with complete understanding.*

8 **Very good user** – *Has fully operational command of the language with only occasional unsystematic inaccuracies and inappropriacies. Misunderstandings may occur in unfamiliar situations. Handles complex detailed argumentation well.*

7 **Good user** – *Has operational command of the language, though with occasional inaccuracies, inappropriacies and misunderstandings in some situations. Generally handles complex language well and understands detailed reasoning.*

6 **Competent user** – *Has generally effective command of the language despite some inaccuracies, inappropriacies and misunderstandings. Can use and understand fairly complex language, particularly in familiar situations.*

5 **Modest user** – *Has partial command of the language, coping with overall meaning in most situations, though is likely to make many mistakes. Should be able to handle basic communication in own field.*

4 **Limited user** – *Basic competence is limited to familiar situations. Has frequent problems in understanding and expression. Is not able to use complex language.*

3 **Extremely limited user** – *Conveys and understands only general meaning in very familiar situations. Frequent breakdowns in communication occur.*

2 **Intermittent user** – *Has great difficulty understanding spoken and written English.*

1 **Non-user** – *Essentially has no ability to use the language beyond possibly a few isolated words.*

0 **Did not attempt the test** – *Did not answer the questions.*

MARKING THE PRACTICE TESTS

Listening and Reading

The answer keys are on pages 121–128.
Each question in the Listening and Reading tests is worth one mark.

Questions which require letter / Roman numeral answers

For questions where the answers are letters or Roman numerals, you should write *only* the number of answers required. For example, if the answer is a single letter or numeral, you should write only one answer. If you have written more letters or numerals than are required, the answer must be marked wrong.

Questions which require answers in the form of words or numbers

- Answers may be written in upper or lower case.
- Words in brackets are *optional* – they are correct, but not necessary.
- Alternative answers are separated by a slash (/).
- If you are asked to write an answer using a certain number of words and/or (a) number(s), you will be penalised if you exceed this. For example, if a question specifies an answer using NO MORE THAN THREE WORDS and the correct answer is 'black leather coat', the answer 'coat of black leather' is *incorrect*.
- In questions where you are expected to complete a gap, you should only transfer the necessary missing word(s) onto the answer sheet. For example, to complete 'in the …', where the correct answer is 'morning', the answer 'in the morning' would be *incorrect*.
- All answers require correct spelling (including words in brackets).
- Both US and UK spelling are acceptable and are included in the answer key.
- All standard alternatives for numbers, dates and currencies are acceptable.
- All standard abbreviations are acceptable.
- You will find additional notes about individual answers in the answer key.

Writing

The sample answers are on pages 129–138. It is not possible for you to give yourself a mark for the Writing tasks. We have provided sample answers (written by candidates), showing their score and the examiners' comments. These sample answers will give you an insight into what is required for the Writing test.

HOW SHOULD YOU INTERPRET YOUR SCORES?

At the end of each Listening and Reading answer key you will find a chart which will help you assess whether, on the basis of your Practice Test results, you are ready to take the IELTS test.

In interpreting your score, there are a number of points you should bear in mind. Your performance in the real IELTS test will be reported in two ways: there will be a Band Score from 1 to 9 for each of the components and an Overall Band Score from 1 to 9, which is the average of your scores in the four components. However, institutions considering your application are advised to look at both the Overall Band Score and the Band Score for each component in order to determine whether you have the language skills needed for a particular course of study or work environment. For example, if you are applying for a course which involves a lot of reading and writing, but no lectures, listening skills might be less important and a score of 5 in Listening might be acceptable if the Overall Band Score was 7. However, for a course which has lots of lectures and spoken instructions, a score of 5 in Listening might be unacceptable even though the Overall Band Score was 7.

Once you have marked your tests, you should have some idea of whether your listening and reading skills are good enough for you to try the IELTS test. If you did well enough in one component, but not in others, you will have to decide for yourself whether you are ready to take the test.

The Practice Tests have been checked to ensure that they are the same level of difficulty as the real IELTS test. However, we cannot guarantee that your score in the Practice Tests will be reflected in the real IELTS test. The Practice Tests can only give you an idea of your possible future performance and it is ultimately up to you to make decisions based on your score.

Different institutions accept different IELTS scores for different types of courses. We have based our recommendations on the average scores which the majority of institutions accept. The institution to which you are applying may, of course, require a higher or lower score than most other institutions.

Test 1

LISTENING

PART 1   *Questions 1–10*

Complete the notes below.

*Write **ONE WORD AND/OR A NUMBER** for each answer.*

Listening test audio

Children's Engineering Workshops

Tiny Engineers (ages 4–5)

Activities

* Create a cover for an **1** .... so they can drop it from a height without breaking it.
* Take part in a competition to build the tallest **2** ....
* Make a **3** .... powered by a balloon.

Junior Engineers (ages 6–8)

Activities:

* Build model cars, trucks and **4** .... and learn how to program them so they can move.
* Take part in a competition to build the longest **5** .... using card and wood.
* Create a short **6** .... with special software.
* Build, **7** .... and program a humanoid robot.

Cost for a five-week block: £50

Held on **8** .... from 10 am to 11 am

Location

Building 10A, **9** .... Industrial Estate, Grasford

Plenty of **10** .... is available.

PART 2   *Questions 11–20*

Listening test audio

Questions 11–14

*Choose the correct letter, **A**, **B** or **C**.*

11 Stevenson's was founded in

   A   1923.
   B   1924.
   C   1926.

12 Originally, Stevenson's manufactured goods for

   A   the healthcare industry.
   B   the automotive industry.
   C   the machine tools industry.

13 What does the speaker say about the company premises?

   A   The company has recently moved.
   B   The company has no plans to move.
   C   The company is going to move shortly.

14 The programme for the work experience group includes

   A   time to do research.
   B   meetings with a teacher.
   C   talks by staff.

Questions 15–20

Label the map below.

*Write the correct letter, **A–J**, next to Questions 15–20.*

Plan of Stevenson's site

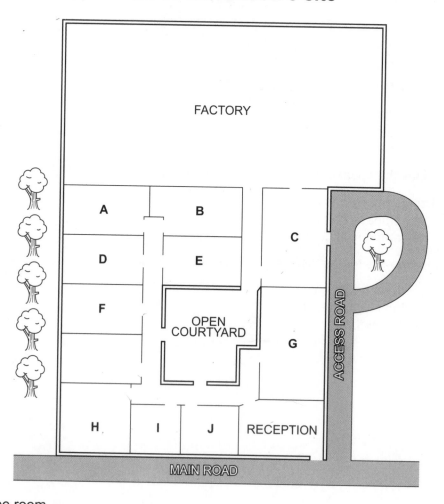

15	coffee room	....
16	warehouse	....
17	staff canteen	....
18	meeting room	....
19	human resources	....
20	boardroom	....

Listening test audio

PART 3   *Questions 21–30*

Questions 21 and 22

*Choose **TWO** letters, **A–E**.*

Which **TWO** parts of the introductory stage to their art projects do Jess and Tom agree were useful?

A   the Bird Park visit
B   the workshop sessions
C   the Natural History Museum visit
D   the projects done in previous years
E   the handouts with research sources

Questions 23 and 24

*Choose **TWO** letters, **A–E**.*

In which **TWO** ways do both Jess and Tom decide to change their proposals?

A   by giving a rationale for their action plans
B   by being less specific about the outcome
C   by adding a video diary presentation
D   by providing a timeline and a mind map
E   by making their notes more evaluative

Questions 25–30

Which personal meaning do the students decide to give to each of the following pictures?

Choose **SIX** answers from the box and write the correct letter, **A–H**, next to Questions 25–30.

Personal meanings
A   a childhood memory
B   hope for the future
C   fast movement
D   a potential threat
E   the power of colour
F   the continuity of life
G   protection of nature
H   a confused attitude to nature

Pictures

25   Falcon (Landseer)   ....

26   Fish hawk (Audubon)   ....

27   Kingfisher (van Gogh)   ....

28   Portrait of William Wells   ....

29   Vairumati (Gauguin)   ....

30   Portrait of Giovanni de Medici   ....

PART 4   *Questions 31–40*

Complete the notes below.

*Write **ONE WORD ONLY** for each answer.*

Listening test audio

Stoicism

Stoicism is still relevant today because of its **31** .... appeal.

Ancient Stoics

- Stoicism was founded over 2,000 years ago in Greece.
- The Stoics' ideas are surprisingly well known, despite not being intended for **32** ....

Stoic principles

- Happiness could be achieved by leading a virtuous life.
- Controlling emotions was essential.
- Epictetus said that external events cannot be controlled but the **33** .... people make in response can be controlled.
- A Stoic is someone who has a different view on experiences which others would consider as **34** ....

The influence of Stoicism

- George Washington organised a **35** .... about Cato to motivate his men.
- The French artist Delacroix was a Stoic.
- Adam Smith's ideas on **36** .... were influenced by Stoicism.
- Some of today's political leaders are inspired by the Stoics.
- Cognitive Behaviour Therapy (CBT)
  – the treatment for **37** .... is based on ideas from Stoicism
  – people learn to base their thinking on **38** ....
- In business, people benefit from Stoicism by identifying obstacles as **39** ....

Relevance of Stoicism

- It requires a lot of **40** .... but Stoicism can help people to lead a good life.
- It teaches people that having a strong character is more important than anything else.

→ 🔊 p. 121   📄 p. 101

READING

SECTION 1   *Questions 1–14*

Read the text below and answer Questions 1–6.

Helping pupils to choose optional subjects when they're aged 14–15: what some pupils say

A   Krishnan

I'm studying Spanish, because it's important to learn foreign languages – and I'm very pleased when I can watch a video in class and understand it. Mr Peckham really pushes us, and offers us extra assignments, to help us improve. That's good for me, because otherwise I'd be quite lazy.

B   Lucy

History is my favourite subject, and it's fascinating to see how what we learn about the past is relevant to what's going on in the world now. It's made me understand much more about politics, for instance. My plan is to study history at university, and maybe go into the diplomatic service, so I can apply a knowledge of history.

C   Mark

Thursdays are my favourite days, because that's when we have computing. It's the high spot of the week for me – I love learning how to program. I began when I was about eight, so when I started doing it at school, I didn't think I'd have any problem with it, but I was quite wrong! When I leave school, I'm going into my family retail business, so sadly I can't see myself becoming a programmer.

D   Violeta

My parents both work in leisure and tourism, and they've always talked about their work a lot at home. I find it fascinating. I'm studying it at school, and the teacher is very knowledgeable, though I think we spend too much time listening to her: I'd like to meet more people working in the sector, and learn from their experience.

E   Walid

I've always been keen on art, so I chose it as an optional subject, though I was afraid the lessons might be a bit dull. I needn't have worried, though – our teacher gets us to do lots of fun things, so there's no risk of getting bored. At the end of the year the class puts on an exhibition for the school, and I'm looking forward to showing some of my work to other people.

Questions 1–6

*Look at the five comments about lessons, **A–E**, on page 16.*

For which comments are the following statements true?

*Write the correct letter, **A–E**, in boxes 1–6 on your answer sheet.*

NB *You may use any letter more than once.*

1   This pupil is interested in the subject despite the way it is taught.

2   This pupil is hoping to have a career that makes use of the subject.

3   This pupil finds the subject harder than they expected.

4   This pupil finds the lessons very entertaining.

5   This pupil appreciates the benefit of doing challenging work.

6   This pupil has realised the connection between two things.

Read the text below and answer Questions 7–14.

It's almost time for the next Ripton Festival!

As usual, the festival will be held in the last weekend of June, this year on Saturday to Monday, 27–29 June. Ever since last year's festival, the committee has been hard at work to make this year's the best ever! The theme is Ripton through the ages. Scenes will be acted out showing how the town has developed since it was first established. But there's also plenty that's up-to-date, from the latest music to local crafts.

The Craft Fair is a regular part of the festival. Come and meet professional artists, designers and craftsmen and women, who will display their jewellery, paintings, ceramics, and much more. They'll also take orders, so if you want one of them to make something especially for you, just ask! You'll get it within a month of the festival ending.

The Saturday barbecue will start at 2 pm and continue until 10 pm, with a bouncy castle for kids. The barbecue will be held in Palmer's Field, or in the town hall if there's rain. Book your tickets now, as they always sell out very quickly! Entry for under 16s is free all day; adults can come for free until 6 pm and pay £5 after that. There'll be live music throughout, with local amateur bands in the afternoon and professional musicians in the evening.

On Sunday we're delighted to introduce an afternoon of boat races, arranged by the Ripton Rowing Club. The spectator area by the bridge has plenty of room to stand and cheer the boats home, in addition to a number of benches. The winners of the races will be presented with trophies by the mayor of Ripton.

All money raised by the festival will go to support the sports clubs in Ripton.

Questions 7–14

Do the following statements agree with the information given in the text on page 18?

In boxes 7–14 on your answer sheet, write

TRUE   *if the statement agrees with the information*
FALSE   *if the statement contradicts the information*
NOT GIVEN   *if there is no information on this*

7   The festival is held every year.

8   This year's festival focuses on the town's history.

9   Goods displayed in the craft fair are unlike ones found in shops.

10   The barbecue will be cancelled if it rains.

11   Adults can attend the barbecue at any time without charge.

12   Amateur musicians will perform during the whole of the barbecue.

13   Seating is available for watching the boat races.

14   People attending the festival will be asked to donate some money.

➜ 🔲 p. 122

SECTION 2   *Questions 15–27*

Read the text below and answer Questions 15–20.

Reducing injuries on the farm

Farms tend to be full of activity. There are always jobs to be done and some tasks require physical manual work. While it is good for people to be active, there are risk factors associated with this, and efforts need to be made to reduce them.

The first risk relates to the carrying of an excessive load or weight. This places undue demands on the spine and can cause permanent damage. Examples of tasks that involve this risk are moving 50-kilogramme fertiliser bags from one site to another or carrying heavy buckets of animal feed around fields. According to the UK Health and Safety Executive, activities such as these 'should be avoided at all times'. Their documentation states that other methods should be considered, such as breaking down the load into smaller containers prior to movement or transporting the materials using a tractor or other vehicle. The risk posed by excessive force is made worse if the person lifting is also bending over as this increases pressure on the discs in the back.

If a load is bulky or hard to grasp, such as a lively or agitated animal, it will be more difficult to hold while lifting and carrying. The holder may adopt an awkward posture, which is tiring and increases the risk of injury. Sometimes a load has to be held away from the body because there is a large obstacle in the area and the person lifting needs to be able to see where their feet are going. This results in increased stress on the back; holding a load at arm's length imposes about five times the stress of a close-to-the-body position. In such cases, handling aids should be purchased that can take the weight off the load and minimise the potential for injury.

Another risk that relates to awkward posture is repetitive bending when carrying out a task. An example might be repairing a gate that has collapsed onto the ground. This type of activity increases the stress on the lower back because the back muscles have to support the weight of the upper body. The farmer should think about whether the job can be performed on a workbench, reducing the need for prolonged awkward posture.

Questions 15–20

Complete the table below.

*Choose **ONE WORD ONLY** from the text on page 20 for each answer.*

Write your answers in boxes 15–20 on your answer sheet.

Risks and how to avoid them		
Risk factor	**Examples of farm activities**	**Risk reduction measures to consider**
Heavy loads	• Lifting sacks of 15 .... • Carrying food for animals	• Divide into containers that weigh less • Use a vehicle such as a tractor
Awkward posture	• Lifting a restless 16 .... • Moving something around a big 17	Buy particular 18 .... to help with support
A lot of 19 .... while working	Fixing a fallen 20	Use a workbench instead

Read the text below and answer Questions 21–27.

Good customer service in retail

Without customers, your retail business would not exist. It stands to reason, therefore, that how you treat your customers has a direct impact on your profit margins.

Some customers just want to browse and not be bothered by sales staff. Try to be sensitive to how much help a customer wants; be proactive in offering help without being annoying. Suggest a product that naturally accompanies what the customer is considering or point out products for which there are special offers, but don't pressure a customer into buying an item they don't want.

Build up a comprehensive knowledge of all the products in your shop, including the pros and cons of products that are alike but that have been produced under a range of brand names. If you have run out of a particular item, make sure you know when the next orders are coming in. Negativity can put customers off instantly. If a customer asks a question to which the answer is 'no', do not just leave it at that – follow it with a positive, for example: 'we're expecting more of that product in on Tuesday'.

Meanwhile, if you see a product in the wrong place on a shelf, don't ignore it – put it back where it belongs. This attention to presentation keeps the shop tidy, giving the right impression to your customers. Likewise, if you notice a fault with a product, remove it and replace it with another.

When necessary, be discreet. For example, if the customer's credit card is declined at the till, keep your voice down and enquire about an alternative payment method quietly so that the customer doesn't feel humiliated. If they experience uncomfortable emotions in your shop, it's unlikely that they'll come back.

Finally, good manners are probably the most important aspect of dealing with customers. Treat each person with respect at all times, even when you are faced with rudeness. Being discourteous yourself will only add more fuel to the fire.

Build a reputation for polite, helpful staff and you'll find that customers not only keep giving you their custom, but also tell their friends about you.

Questions 21–27

Complete the sentences below.

Choose **NO MORE THAN TWO WORDS** *from the text on page 22 for each answer.*

Write your answers in boxes 21–27 on your answer sheet.

21 A .... approach to selling is fine as long as you do not irritate the customer.

22 Recommend additional products and .... without being too forceful.

23 Know how to compare similar products which have different ....

24 Avoid .... by always saying more than 'no'.

25 Keep an eye on the .... of goods on the shelves.

26 If a customer has problems paying with their .... , handle the problem with care.

27 Any .... from a customer should not affect how you treat them.

→ 🔊 p. 122

SECTION 3 *Questions 28–40*

Read the text on pages 25 and 26 and answer Questions 28–40.

Questions 28–34

The text on pages 25 and 26 has seven paragraphs, **A–G**.

Choose the correct heading for each paragraph from the list of headings below.

Write the correct number, i–viii, in boxes 28–34 on your answer sheet.

List of Headings

i   A time when opportunities were limited

ii   The reasons why Ferrando's product is needed

iii   A no-risk solution

iv   Two inventions and some physical details

v   The contrasting views of different generations

vi   A disturbing experience

vii   The problems with replacing a consumer item

viii   Looking back at why water was bottled

---

28   Paragraph **A**

29   Paragraph **B**

30   Paragraph **C**

31   Paragraph **D**

32   Paragraph **E**

33   Paragraph **F**

34   Paragraph **G**

Plastic is no longer fantastic

A   In 2017, Carlos Ferrando, a Spanish engineer-turned-entrepreneur, saw a piece of art in a museum that profoundly affected him. 'What Lies Under', a photographic composition by Indonesian digital artist Ferdi Rizkiyanto, shows a child crouching by the edge of the ocean and 'lifting up' a wave, to reveal a cluster of assorted plastic waste, from polyethylene bags to water bottles. The artwork, designed to raise public awareness, left Ferrando angry – and fuelled with entrepreneurial ideas.

B   Ferrando runs a Spanish-based design company, Closca, that produces an ingenious foldable bicycle helmet. But he has now also designed a stylish glass water bottle with a stretchy silicone strap and magnetic closure mechanism that means it can be attached to almost anything, from a bike to a bag to a pushchair handle. The product comes with an app that tells people where they can fill their bottles with water for free.

C   The intention is to persuade people to stop buying water in plastic bottles, thus saving consumers money and reducing the plastic waste piling up in our oceans. 'Bottled water is now a $100 billion business, and 81 per cent of the bottles are not recycled. It's a complete waste – water is only 1.5 per cent of the price of the bottle!' Ferrando cries. Indeed, environmentalists estimate that by 2050 there will be more plastic in our oceans than fish and that's mainly down to such bottles. 'We are trying to create a sense that being environmentally sophisticated is a status symbol,' he adds. 'We want people to clip their bottles onto what they are wearing, to show that they are recycling – and to look cool.'

D   Ferrando's story is fascinating because it seems like an indicator of something unexpected. Three decades ago, conspicuous consumption – the purchase of luxuries, such as handbags, shoes, cars, etc. on a lavish scale – heightened people's social status. Indeed, the closing decades of the 20th century were a time when it seemed that anything could be turned into a commodity. Hence the fact that water became a consumer item, sold in plastic bottles, instead of just emerging, for free, from a tap.

E   Today, though, conspicuous extravagance no longer seems desirable among consumers. Now, recycling is fashionable – as is cycling rather than driving. Plastic water bottles have become so common that they do not command status; instead, what many millennials – young people born in the late 20th century – prefer to post on social media are 'real' (refillable) bottles or even the once widespread Thermos bottles. Some teenagers currently think that these stainless-steel vacuum-insulated water bottles that are coming back onto the market are ultra 'cool'; never mind the fact that they feel oddly out-of-date to anyone over the age of 40 or that teenagers in the 1970s would have avoided ever being seen with one.

F   It is uncertain whether Closca will succeed in its goal. Although its foldable bike helmet is available in some outlets in New York, including the Museum of Modern Art, it can be very hard for any design entrepreneur to really take off in the global mass market, though not as hard as it might have been in the past. If an entrepreneur had wanted to fund a smart invention a few decades ago, he or she would have had to either raise a bank loan, borrow money from a family member or use a credit card. Things have moved on slightly since then.

G   Entrepreneurs are still using the last two options, but some are also tapping into the ever-growing pot of money that is becoming available in the management world for 'corporate social responsibility' (CSR) investments. And then there are other options for those who wish to raise money straight away. Ferrando posted details about his water-bottle venture on a large, recognised platform for funding creative projects. He appealed for people to donate $30,000 of seed money – the money he needed to get his project going – and promised to give a bottle to anyone who provided more than $39 in 'donations'. If he received the funds, he stated that the company would produce bottles in grey and white; if $60,000 was raised, a multicoloured one would be made. Using this approach, none of the donors has a stake in his idea, nor does he have any debt. Instead, it is almost a pre-sale of the product, in a manner that tests demand in advance and creates a potential crowd of enthusiasts. This old-fashioned community funding with a digital twist is supporting a growing array of projects ranging from films to card games, videos, watches and so on. And, at last count, Closca had raised some $52,838 from 803 backers. Maybe, 20 years from now, it will be the plastic bottle that seems peculiarly old-fashioned.

Questions 35–37

*Choose the correct letter, **A**, **B**, **C** or **D**.*

Write the correct letter in boxes 35–37 on your answer sheet.

35   What does Ferrando say about his glass water bottle?

    A   It matches his bicycle helmet.
    B   It is cheaper than a plastic bottle.
    C   He has designed it to suit all ages.
    D   He wants people to be proud to show it.

36   What does the writer find fascinating about Ferrando's story?

    A   the youthfulness of his ideas
    B   the old-fashioned nature of his products
    C   the choice it is creating for consumers
    D   the change it is revealing in people's attitudes

37   What does the writer suggest about Closca's bike helmet?

    A   It has both functional and artistic value.
    B   Its main appeal is to older people.
    C   It has had extraordinary success worldwide.
    D   It is a more exciting invention than the glass bottle.

Questions 38–40

Complete the summary below.

*Choose **ONE WORD ONLY** from the text on pages 25 and 26 for each answer.*

Write your answers in boxes 38–40 on your answer sheet.

Funding a smart invention

Thirty years ago, the methods used by creators to fund their projects involved getting money from the bank or from someone in the **38** .... Banks today are still a useful source of finance, but investments may also be sought from 'corporate social responsibility' projects.

In order to get immediate funding, the method Ferrando took was to use a well-known **39** .... to advertise his product and request financial support. People who gave a certain figure or over were offered a free gift. In addition, Ferrando advised his donors that his company would create bottles in two colours, followed by a **40** .... bottle once they had received a more significant amount. In this way, Ferrando avoided debt and found out how many people might want his products before manufacturing them.

WRITING

WRITING TASK 1

You should spend about 20 minutes on this task.

> *Mrs Barrett, an English-speaking woman who lives in your town, has advertised for someone to help her in her home for a few hours a day next summer.*
>
> *Write a letter to Mrs Barrett. In your letter*
> - *suggest how you could help her in her home*
> - *say why you would like to do this work*
> - *explain when you will and will not be available*

Write at least 150 words.

You do **NOT** need to write any addresses.

Begin your letter as follows:

Dear Mrs Barrett,

→ 🖉 p. 129

WRITING TASK 2

You should spend about 40 minutes on this task.

Write about the following topic:

> **Plastic bags, plastic bottles and plastic packaging are bad for the environment.**
>
> **What damage does plastic do to the environment?**
>
> **What can be done by governments and individuals to solve this problem?**

Give reasons for your answer and include any relevant examples from your own knowledge or experience.

Write at least 250 words.

SPEAKING

PART 1

The examiner asks you about yourself, your home, work or studies and other familiar topics.

EXAMPLE

Example Speaking test video

People you study/work with

- Who do you spend most time studying/working with? [Why?]
- What kinds of things do you study / work on with other people? [Why?]
- Are there times when you study/work better by yourself? [Why/Why not?]
- Is it important to like the people you study/work with? [Why/Why not?]

PART 2

> **Describe a tourist attraction you enjoyed visiting.**
>
> **You should say:**
> **what this tourist attraction is**
> **when and why you visited it**
> **what you did there**
>
> **and explain why you enjoyed visiting this tourist attraction.**

You will have to talk about the topic for one to two minutes. You have one minute to think about what you are going to say. You can make some notes to help you if you wish.

PART 3

Discussion topics:

Different kinds of tourist attractions

Example questions:
What are the most popular tourist attractions in your country?
How do the types of tourist attractions that younger people like to visit compare with those that older people like to visit?
Do you agree that some tourist attractions (e.g. national museums/galleries) should be free to visit?

The importance of international tourism

Example questions:
Why is tourism important to a country?
What are the benefits to individuals of visiting another country as tourists?
How necessary is it for tourists to learn the language of the country they're visiting?

Test 2

LISTENING

PART 1   *Questions 1–10*

Complete the table below.

*Write **ONE WORD AND/OR A NUMBER** for each answer.*

Listening test audio

Copying photos to digital format
Name of company: Picturerep
Requirements   • Maximum size of photos is 30 cm, minimum size 4 cm.   • Photos must not be in a **1** .... or an album.
Cost   • The cost for 360 photos is **2** £ .... (including one disk).   • Before the completed order is sent, **3** .... is required.
Services included in the price   • Photos can be placed in a folder, e.g. with the name **4** ....   • The **5** .... and contrast can be improved if necessary.   • Photos which are very fragile will be scanned by **6** ....
Special restore service (costs extra)   • It may be possible to remove an object from a photo, or change the   **7** ....   • A photo which is not correctly in **8** .... cannot be fixed.
Other information   • Orders are completed within **9** ....   • Send the photos in a box (not **10** ....).

PART 2   *Questions 11–20*

Questions 11–15

*Choose the correct letter, **A**, **B** or **C**.*

Listening test audio

11 Dartfield House school used to be

    A   a tourist information centre.
    B   a private home.
    C   a local council building.

12 What is planned with regard to the lower school?

    A   All buildings on the main site will be improved.
    B   The lower school site will be used for new homes.
    C   Additional school buildings will be constructed on the lower school site.

13 The catering has been changed because of

    A   long queuing times.
    B   changes to the school timetable.
    C   dissatisfaction with the menus.

14 Parents are asked to

    A   help their children to decide in advance which serving point to use.
    B   make sure their children have enough money for food.
    C   advise their children on healthy food to eat.

15 What does the speaker say about the existing canteen?

    A   Food will still be served there.
    B   Only staff will have access to it.
    C   Pupils can take their food into it.

Questions 16–18

What comment does the speaker make about each of the following serving points in the Food Hall?

*Choose **THREE** answers from the box and write the correct letter, **A–D**, next to Questions 16–18.*

```
┌─────────────────────────────────────────┐
│              Comments                     │
│                                           │
│   A    pupils help to plan menus          │
│                                           │
│   B    only vegetarian food               │
│                                           │
│   C    different food every week          │
│                                           │
│   D    daily change in menu               │
│                                           │
└─────────────────────────────────────────┘
```

Food available at serving points in Food Hall

16   World Adventures   ....

17   Street Life   ....

18   Speedy Italian   ....

Questions 19 and 20

*Choose **TWO** letters, **A–E**.*

Which **TWO** optional after-school lessons are new?

    A   swimming
    B   piano
    C   acting
    D   cycling
    E   theatre sound and lighting

PART 3   *Questions 21–30*

Questions 21–24

*Choose the correct letter, **A**, **B** or **C**.*

Listening test audio

Assignment on sleep and dreams

21 Luke read that one reason why we often forget dreams is that

    A   our memories cannot cope with too much information.
    B   we might otherwise be confused about what is real.
    C   we do not think they are important.

22 What do Luke and Susie agree about dreams predicting the future?

    A   It may just be due to chance.
    B   It only happens with certain types of event.
    C   It happens more often than some people think.

23 Susie says that a study on pre-school children having a short nap in the day

    A   had controversial results.
    B   used faulty research methodology.
    C   failed to reach any clear conclusions.

24 In their last assignment, both students had problems with

    A   statistical analysis.
    B   making an action plan.
    C   self-assessment.

Questions 25–30

Complete the flow chart below.

*Write **ONE WORD ONLY** for each answer.*

Assignment plan

Decide on research question:

Is there a relationship between hours of sleep and number of dreams?

⬇

Decide on sample:

Twelve students from the **25** .... department

⬇

Decide on methodology:

Self-reporting

⬇

Decide on procedure:

Answers on **26** ....

⬇

Check ethical guidelines for working with **27** ....

Ensure that risk is assessed and **28** .... is kept to a minimum

⬇

Analyse the results

Calculate the correlation and make a **29** ....

⬇

---

30 .... the research

PART 4   *Questions 31–40*

Complete the notes below.

*Write **ONE WORD ONLY** for each answer.*

Listening test audio

Health benefits of dance

Recent findings:

- All forms of dance produce various hormones associated with feelings of happiness.

- Dancing with others has a more positive impact than dancing alone.

- An experiment on university students suggested that dance increases **31** ....

- For those with mental illness, dance could be used as a form of **32** ....

Benefits of dance for older people:

- accessible for people with low levels of **33** ....

- reduces the risk of heart disease

- better **34** .... reduces the risk of accidents

- improves **35** .... function by making it work faster

- improves participants' general well-being

- gives people more **36** .... to take exercise

- can lessen the feeling of **37** .... , very common in older people

Benefits of Zumba:

- A study at The University of Wisconsin showed that doing Zumba for 40 minutes uses up as many **38** .... as other quite intense forms of exercise.

- The *American Journal of Health Behavior* study showed that:

  – women suffering from **39** .... benefited from doing Zumba.

  – Zumba became a **40** .... for the participants.

→ 🔲 p. 123 📄 p. 107

READING

SECTION 1   *Questions 1–14*

Read the text below and answer Questions 1–7.

How to choose your builder

Building a new home is a significant investment, and it's essential to find the right builder for the job. Before you look for a builder, it's important to develop a comprehensive budget and have clear plans. Once you have a design in mind, it is time to start narrowing down your builder shortlist, and this starts with assessing how qualified each builder is. In Australia, this means checking that the builder holds a residential building licence. Most states have their own building authority who you can contact to check a builder's licence.

You can also check if the builder is a member of an industry association such as the Housing Industry Association (HIA), and whether they have won any industry awards. For instance, the HIA runs a state and national awards programme, with a category that recognises the level of customer service that a builder delivers.

Most experts agree that display homes (homes constructed by the builder that are open to the public) offer a great opportunity to study their work up close. Display homes are usually offered by major project builders who work on a large scale and can deliver good quality and value. You can also talk to the salesperson and find out about the home design and what is and isn't included in the sale price. And it may be possible to talk to other customers you meet there and ask their opinion of the workmanship in the display home.

Finally, avoid signing any business contract before you have read and understood it thoroughly. Ask your builder to use a standard building contract that has been designed to comply with the Domestic Building Contracts Act, and to be fair to both client and builder. You have five business days within which you may withdraw from the contract after signing it.

Questions 1–7

Do the following statements agree with the information given in the text on page 38?

In boxes 1–7 on your answer sheet, write

> **TRUE**   *if the statement agrees with the information*
> **FALSE**   *if the statement contradicts the information*
> **NOT GIVEN** *if there is no information on this*

1   After selecting a builder, you should decide on the design of your new house.

2   In Australia, you can make sure that a builder has the appropriate licence.

3   The best builders usually belong to the Housing Industry Association.

4   The HIA gives an award to builders whose standards of customer service are very high.

5   Builders who work on smaller projects are more likely to have display homes.

6   It is advisable to have a contract which is in accordance with the Domestic Building Contracts Act.

7   A contract is legally binding from the time it has been signed.

Read the text below and answer Questions 8–14.

Island adventure activities

A   Rib riding

Conquer stormy seas on a high-speed ride in an RIB (Rigid Inflatable Boat). These powerful boats cut through choppy waters with ease. You'll need to hold on tight as the boat bounces across the wake of awesome cruise liners in one of the world's busiest shipping lanes.

B   Horse riding

Experience the thrill of riding on horseback along peaceful country lanes and secluded bridleways with the help of expert guides. Even a novice can quickly take the reins and feel the thrill of riding one of nature's most magnificent beasts.

C   Kayaking

Test your kayak nerves paddling around a deserted military fort built on a rocky outcrop out at sea, then explore the island's busy harbours before gliding back to dry land where a hot shower and a cup of tea await.

D   Cycling

Test your endurance on the famous Round the Island Cycle Route. Grit your teeth and tackle the brutal hills in the south of the island, or for something less challenging, discover our car-free cycle tracks on former railway lines.

E   Segway riding

Have you got what it takes to master a Segway? In theory, these quirky electric machines are simple to control, with users leaning forwards to go faster and back to slow down. In reality, you'll need some practice before you can master the skill and glide around the island.

F   Tree climbing

A climb into the canopy of a 25-metre oak tree is an amazing experience. Supported by a rope and harness, you can stand on branches no bigger than your wrist, and swing out between the boughs, or simply take the opportunity to lie in a tree-top hammock and absorb the stunning bird's eye views.

G   Coasteering

Tackle the spectacular coast in the north of the island. Scrabble over the rocks around cliff edges as the waves crash around you, dive through submerged caves and emerge onto a beach once used by smugglers. This is a thrilling experience, but not an adventure to attempt alone.

H   Mountain boarding

First developed as an off-season alternative to winter sports and now a sport in its own right, mountain boarding has the speed of snowboarding but with a harder landing when you fall. After a bit of practice and a few bruises, you'll learn to control the ride and can join the few people who can call themselves mountain boarders.

Questions 8–14

*Look at the eight advertisements for adventure sports on an island, **A–H**, on page 40.*

For which adventure sport are the following statements true?

*Write the correct letter, **A–H**, in boxes 8–14 on your answer sheet.*

NB *You may use any letter more than once.*

   8   You will be provided with safety equipment.

   9   You may get some minor injuries doing this activity.

 10   You can see a disused, isolated building.

 11   You can relax and look down from above in an unusual location.

 12   You will take an exciting trip in rough water close to big ships.

 13   You can choose easy options or more difficult ones.

 14   You may find this more difficult than you expect.

→ ◐ p. 124

SECTION 2   *Questions 15–27*

Read the text below and answer Questions 15–20.

Barrington Music Service:
Business and Development Manager

Barrington Music Service organises a wide range of music activities for children and young people resident in and around Barrington. It provides singing and specialist instrumental lessons in schools, and it owns a collection of instruments for use in schools, some of which are available for hire by the parents of children having lessons. The Service also arranges a number of music-related events, including festivals bringing together choirs and soloists from schools in both Barrington and other areas. The Music Service provides administrative and financial support for the Barrington Youth Orchestra, which takes part in workshops with professional artists and gives performances.

Barrington Music Service is seeking to recruit a Business and Development Manager to manage the administrative function and build on the success of the Service. We are looking for an individual with a passion for delivering the best possible music provision for the benefit of our children and young people.

As the Business and Development Manager, you will be responsible for managing the administrative and financial systems of the Music Service, ensuring it does not exceed its budget, which is currently around £1m a year. You will take the lead on marketing the Service and ensuring the generation of new income. The Music Service is involved in several partnerships with schools and with music and community organisations in the district, and you will be expected to increase the number and scope of these, as well as take the lead in fundraising. The Service recently embarked on a programme to broaden what is taught in school music lessons, to include instruments and musical styles from around the world, and you will be required to further develop this emphasis on diversity.

You will need to improve systems for ensuring that the records of the Service's activities are accurate, and maintain a database of all music teachers, students, and instruments belonging to the Service.

The person appointed will have experience of a supervisory role and the skills to motivate members of a team. You will have an understanding of accounting, at a non-specialist level, and of standard financial procedures. High-level IT skills and excellent verbal and written communication skills are essential. Although experience in music education is not crucial, good knowledge of the field, or of other areas of arts management, would be an advantage.

Questions 15–20

Complete the notes below.

*Choose **ONE WORD ONLY** from the text on page 42 for each answer.*

Write your answers in boxes 15–20 on your answer sheet.

Barrington Music Service

Activities

- organises music lessons
- enables the hire of instruments
- events such as **15** .... for local and visiting schools
- supports Barrington Youth Orchestra

Post of Business and Development Manager

Person appointed will

- manage the administration of the Service
- be responsible for keeping to the **16** ....
- build **17** .... with other organisations
- be proactive in fundraising
- increase the focus on **18** .... in school music lessons (e.g., international styles)
- make sure records and a **19** .... is kept up-to-date

Person appointed must have

- ability to supervise and motivate others
- basic knowledge of **20** ....
- other relevant skills

Read the text below and answer Questions 21–27.

Health and safety in small businesses

The rate of accidents at work is almost 75% higher in small businesses than in larger companies. One possible reason is that many managers of small businesses have an inadequate knowledge of health and safety issues.

Many managers of small businesses claim their situation is made worse by bureaucracy, arguing that the huge number of regulations – not just on health and safety but also on tax, the minimum wage, and much, much more – makes their work difficult.

Many managers are simply not aware of their responsibilities. They are too busy running their companies to read manuals, employ consultants or go to seminars. Moreover, the average business person doesn't know where and how to get information.

The Federation of Small Businesses argues that the special nature of small businesses should be recognised by health and safety inspectors, with an emphasis on education and how to comply with the law, rather than simply on enforcement. For instance, inspectors could make employers aware of what they really need to know, rather than swamping them with mountains of leaflets which may not be relevant.

Improvements are being made, however. The Health and Safety Executive has issued a free guide to the most important health and safety laws for employers. All employers must have their own health and safety policy statement and, for businesses with more than five employees, this must be in writing. It should be specific to the business and clear about the arrangements for and organisation of health and safety at work.

It should state a strategy, detail how it will be implemented and by whom, and say when it will be reviewed and updated. It is advisable to involve employees in this process, as they have direct experience.

Assessing and identifying risks is the starting point. But to comply with the law, businesses must train their employees about health and safety, and provide information to others who need to know, such as the contractors working for them. These are often smaller companies that carry out most of the dangerous work. Helping them to get into good safety habits makes it easier for them to tender for work from big companies.

Other advice from the Health and Safety Executive for small businesses tackles specific issues, such as helping small companies to deal with work-related stress.

Questions 21–27

Complete the sentences below.

*Choose **ONE WORD ONLY** from the text on page 44 for each answer.*

Write your answers in boxes 21–27 on your answer sheet.

21 One cause of health and safety problems in small businesses is that managers do not have enough relevant ....

22 Managers complain they have too many .... to deal with.

23 Managers may not fully understand their ....

24 Businesses sometimes feel that inspectors give them far too many

....

25 Businesses above a certain size must produce a written .... of their health and safety policy.

26 A company's health and safety policy is relevant to both its employees and its ....

27 The Health and Safety Executive can advise small businesses on problems of .... among their employees.

SECTION 3   *Questions 28–40*

Read the text below and answer Questions 28–40.

Jobs in ancient Egypt

In order to be engaged in the higher professions in ancient Egypt, a person had to be literate and so first had to become a scribe. The apprenticeship for this job lasted many years and was tough and challenging. It principally involved memorizing hieroglyphic symbols and practicing handwritten lettering. Scribes noted the everyday activities in ancient Egypt and wrote about everything from grain stocks to tax records. Therefore, most of our information on this rich culture comes from their records. Most scribes were men from privileged backgrounds. The occupation of scribe was among the most sought-after in ancient Egypt. Craftspeople endeavored to get their sons into the school for scribes, but they were rarely successful.

As in many civilizations, the lower classes provided the means for those above them to live comfortable lives. You needed to work if you wanted to eat, but there was no shortage of jobs at any time in Egypt's history. The commonplace items taken for granted today, such as a brush or bowl, had to be made by hand; laundry had to be washed by hand, clothing sewn, and sandals made from papyrus and palm leaves. In order to make these and have paper to write on, papyrus plants had to be harvested, processed, and distributed and all these jobs needed workers. There were rewards and sometimes difficulties. The reed cutter, for example, who harvested papyrus plants along the Nile, had to bear in mind that he worked in an area that was also home to wildlife that, at times, could prove fatal.

At the bottom rung of all these jobs were the people who served as the basis for the entire economy: the farmers. Farmers usually did not own the land they worked. They were given food, implements, and living quarters as payment for their labor. Although there were many more glamorous jobs than farming, farmers were the backbone of the Egyptian economy and sustained everyone else.

The details of lower-class jobs are known from medical reports on the treatment of injuries, letters, and documents written on various professions, literary works, tomb inscriptions, and artistic representations. This evidence presents a comprehensive view of daily work in ancient Egypt – how the jobs were done, and sometimes how people felt about the work. In general, the Egyptians seem to have felt pride in their work no matter what their occupation. Everyone had something to contribute to the community, and no skills seem to have been considered non-essential. The potter who produced cups and bowls was as important to the community as the scribe, and the amulet-maker as vital as the pharmacist.

Part of making a living, regardless of one's special skills, was taking part in the king's monumental building projects. Although it is commonly believed that the great monuments and temples of Egypt were achieved through slave labor, there is absolutely no evidence to support this. The pyramids and other monuments were built by Egyptian laborers who either donated their time as community service or were paid for their labor, and Egyptians from every occupation could be called on to do this.

Stone had to first be quarried and this required workers to split the blocks from the rock cliffs. It was done by inserting wooden wedges in the rock which would swell and cause the stone to break from the face. The often huge blocks were then pushed onto sleds, devices better suited than wheeled vehicles to moving weighty objects over shifting sand. They were then rolled to a different location where they could be cut and shaped. This job was done by skilled stonemasons working with copper chisels and wooden mallets. As the chisels could get blunt, a specialist in sharpening would take the tool, sharpen it, and bring it back. This would have been constant daily work as the masons could wear down their tools on a single block.

The blocks were then moved into position by unskilled laborers. These people were mostly farmers who could do nothing with their land during the months when the Nile River overflowed its banks. Egyptologists Bob Brier and Hoyt Hobbs explain: 'For two months annually, workmen gathered by the tens of thousands from all over the country to transport the blocks a permanent crew had quarried during the rest of the year. Overseers organized the men into teams to transport the stones on the sleds.' Once the pyramid was complete, the inner chambers needed to be decorated by scribes who painted elaborate images on the walls. Interior work on tombs and temples also required sculptors who could expertly cut away the stone around certain figures or scenes that had been painted.

While these artists were highly skilled, everyone – no matter what their job for the rest of the year – was expected to contribute to communal projects. This practice was in keeping with the value of *ma'at* (harmony and balance) which was central to Egyptian culture. One was expected to care for others as much as oneself and contributing to the common good was an expression of this. There is no doubt there were many people who did not love their job every day, but the Egyptian government was aware of how hard the people worked and so staged a number of festivals throughout the year to show gratitude and give them days off to relax.

Questions 28–32

*Choose the correct letter, **A**, **B**, **C** or **D**.*

Write the correct letter in boxes 28–32 on your answer sheet.

28   What does the writer say about scribes in ancient Egypt?

      A   Their working days were very long.
      B   The topics they wrote about were very varied.
      C   Many of them were once ordinary working people.
      D   Few of them realised the true value of their occupation.

29   What is the writer doing in the second paragraph?

      A   explaining why jobs were plentiful in ancient Egypt
      B   pointing out how honest workers were in ancient Egypt
      C   comparing manual and professional work in ancient Egypt
      D   noting the range of duties an individual worker had in ancient Egypt

30   What is the writer doing in the fifth paragraph?

      A   explaining a problem
      B   describing a change
      C   rejecting a popular view
      D   criticising a past activity

31   The writer refers to the value of *ma'at* in order to explain

      A   how the work of artists reflected beliefs in ancient Egypt.
      B   how ancient Egyptians viewed their role in society.
      C   why the opinions of certain people were valued in ancient Egypt.
      D   why ancient Egyptians expressed their views so readily.

32   Which word best describes the attitude of the Egyptian government toward its workers?

      A   strict
      B   patient
      C   negligent
      D   appreciative

Questions 33–36

Look at the following statements (Questions 33–36) and the list of jobs below.

*Match each statement with the correct job, **A–G**.*

*Write the correct letter, **A–G**, in boxes 33–36 on your answer sheet.*

33   was unable to work at certain times

34   divided workers into groups

35   faced daily hazards

36   underwent a long period of training

List of Jobs

A   scribe

B   reed cutter

C   farmer

D   potter

E   stonemason

F   overseer

G   sculptor

Questions 37–40

Complete the summary below.

*Choose **NO MORE THAN TWO WORDS** from the text on pages 46 and 47 for each answer.*

Write your answers in boxes 37–40 on your answer sheet.

The king's building projects

Labourers who worked on the king's buildings were local people who chose to participate in **37** .... or who received payment.

The work involved breaking up stone cliffs using wooden wedges. The large pieces of stone were then transported to another site on sleds, which moved easily over the **38** .... Here, the blocks could be cut and shaped using tools made of **39** .... and wood. Some of these had to be sharpened regularly.

Eventually, the stone was moved into place to create a building. The job of moving the stone was often done by **40** .... or other unskilled workers.

WRITING TASK 1

You should spend about 20 minutes on this task.

You have just read an article in a national newspaper which claims that town centres in your country all look very similar to each other. You don't fully agree with this opinion.

Write a letter to the editor of the newspaper. In your letter

- *say which points in the article you agree with*

- *explain ways in which your town centre is different from most other town centres*

- *offer to give a guided tour of your town to the writer of the article*

Write at least 150 words.

You do **NOT** need to write any addresses.

Begin your letter as follows:

Dear Sir or Madam,

→ 🖉 p. 132   51

WRITING TASK 2

You should spend about 40 minutes on this task.

Write about the following topic:

> *Some people like to try new things, for example, places to visit and types of food. Other people prefer to keep doing things they are familiar with.*
>
> *Discuss both these attitudes and give your own opinion.*

Give reasons for your answer and include any relevant examples from your own knowledge or experience.

Write at least 250 words.

PART 1

The examiner asks you about yourself, your home, work or studies and other familiar topics.

EXAMPLE

Flowers and plants

- Do you have a favourite flower or plant? [Why/Why not?]
- What kinds of flowers and plants grow near where you live? [Why/Why not?]
- Is it important to you to have flowers and plants in your home? [Why/Why not?]
- Have you ever bought flowers for someone else? [Why/Why not?]

PART 2

Describe a review you read about a product or service.

You should say:
>   **where you read the review**
>   **what the product or service was**
>   **what information the review gave about the product or service**

and explain what you did as a result of reading this review.

You will have to talk about the topic for one to two minutes. You have one minute to think about what you are going to say. You can make some notes to help you if you wish.

PART 3

Discussion topics:

Online reviews

Example questions:
What kinds of things do people write online reviews about in your country?
Why do some people write online reviews?
Do you think that online reviews are good for both shoppers and companies?

Customer service

Example questions:
What do you think it might be like to work in a customer service job?
Do you agree that customers are more likely to complain nowadays?
How important is it for companies to take all customer complaints seriously?

Test 3

PART 1   *Questions 1–10*

Complete the notes below.

Write ONE WORD AND/OR A NUMBER for each answer.

Listening test audio

JUNIOR CYCLE CAMP
The course focuses on skills and safety.

- Charlie would be placed in Level 5.
- First of all, children at this level are taken to practise in a **1** ....

Instructors

- Instructors wear **2** .... shirts.
- A **3** .... is required and training is given.

Classes

- The size of the classes is limited.
- There are quiet times during the morning for a **4** .... or a game.
- Classes are held even if there is **5** ....

What to bring

- a change of clothing
- a **6** ....
- shoes (not sandals)
- Charlie's **7** ....

Day 1

- Charlie should arrive at 9.20 am on the first day.
- Before the class, his **8** .... will be checked.
- He should then go to the **9** .... to meet his class instructor.

Cost

- The course costs **10** $ .... per week.

PART 2   *Questions 11–20*

Questions 11 and 12

*Choose **TWO** letters, **A–E**.*

Listening test audio

According to Megan, what are the **TWO** main advantages of working in the agriculture and horticulture sectors?

    A   the active lifestyle
    B   the above-average salaries
    C   the flexible working opportunities
    D   the opportunities for overseas travel
    E   the chance to be in a natural environment

Questions 13 and 14

*Choose **TWO** letters, **A–E**.*

Which **TWO** of the following are likely to be disadvantages for people working outdoors?

    A   the increasing risk of accidents
    B   being in a very quiet location
    C   difficult weather conditions at times
    D   the cost of housing
    E   the level of physical fitness required

Questions 15–20

What information does Megan give about each of the following job opportunities?

*Choose **SIX** answers from the box and write the correct letter, **A–H**, next to Questions 15–20.*

Information

A   not a permanent job

B   involves leading a team

C   experience not essential

D   intensive work but also fun

E   chance to earn more through overtime

F   chance for rapid promotion

G   accommodation available

H   local travel involved

Job opportunities

15 Fresh food commercial manager   ....

16 Agronomist   ....

17 Fresh produce buyer   ....

18 Garden centre sales manager   ....

19 Tree technician   ....

20 Farm worker   ....

PART 3   *Questions 21–30*

Questions 21 and 22

Choose TWO letters, A–E.

Listening test audio

Which **TWO** points does Adam make about his experiment on artificial sweeteners?

A	The results were what he had predicted.
B	The experiment was simple to set up.
C	A large sample of people was tested.
D	The subjects were unaware of what they were drinking.
E	The test was repeated several times for each person.

Questions 23 and 24

Choose TWO letters, A–E.

Which **TWO** problems did Rosie have when measuring the fat content of nuts?

A	She used the wrong sort of nuts.
B	She used an unsuitable chemical.
C	She did not grind the nuts finely enough.
D	The information on the nut package was incorrect.
E	The weighing scales may have been unsuitable.

Questions 25–30

*Choose the correct letter, **A**, **B** or **C**.*

25 Adam suggests that restaurants could reduce obesity if their menus

    A   offered fewer options.
    B   had more low-calorie foods.
    C   were organised in a particular way.

26 The students agree that food manufacturers deliberately

    A   make calorie counts hard to understand.
    B   fail to provide accurate calorie counts.
    C   use ineffective methods to reduce calories.

27 What does Rosie say about levels of exercise in England?

    A   The amount recommended is much too low.
    B   Most people overestimate how much they do.
    C   Women now exercise more than they used to.

28 Adam refers to the location and width of stairs in a train station to illustrate

    A   practical changes that can influence people's behaviour.
    B   methods of helping people who have mobility problems.
    C   ways of preventing accidents by controlling crowd movement.

29 What do the students agree about including reference to exercise in their presentation?

    A   They should probably leave it out.
    B   They need to do more research on it.
    C   They should discuss this with their tutor.

30 What are the students going to do next for their presentation?

    A   prepare some slides for it
    B   find out how long they have for it
    C   decide on its content and organisation

PART 4   *Questions 31–40*

Complete the notes below.

*Write **ONE WORD ONLY** for each answer.*

Listening test audio

Hand knitting

Interest in knitting

- Knitting has a long history around the world.
- We imagine someone like a **31** .... knitting.
- A **32** .... ago, knitting was expected to disappear.
- The number of knitting classes is now increasing.
- People are buying more **33** .... for knitting nowadays.

Benefits of knitting

- gives support in times of **34** .... difficulty
- requires only **35** .... skills and little money to start
- reduces stress in a busy life

Early knitting

- The origins are not known.
- Findings show early knitted items to be **36** .... in shape.
- The first needles were made of natural materials such as wood and **37** ....
- Early yarns felt **38** .... to touch.
- Wool became the most popular yarn for spinning.
- Geographical areas had their own **39** .... of knitting.
- Everyday tasks like looking after **40** .... were done while knitting.

READING

SECTION 1   *Questions 1–14*

Read the text below and answer Questions 1–5.

Maps showing walks starting from Bingham Town Hall

A   The walk described in this leaflet takes you to one of the many places in the district where bricks were made for hundreds of years, until it was closed in the late 19th century. This brickworks is now the largest and best-known nature reserve in the area. Please note that the ground is very uneven, and under-sixes should not be taken on this walk.

B   This walk will take you to the top of Burley Hill, along a nice easy path that people of all ages will be able to manage. From the summit you can see for a great distance to the north and west, across a landscape that includes half a dozen lakes and the entrance to Butter Caves. Bear in mind, though, that mist often comes in from the sea and covers the hilltop.

C   This route leads you through the village of Cottesloe, which was created in the 1930s and is famous for its strange-looking houses and ceramics factory, which is still the largest employer in the area. An artificial lake was originally created beside the village, and has since been filled in and turned into an adventure playground. After you leave Cottesloe, you have a choice of routes to return to the starting point, so either continue via Thurley Park, or if it's raining, take the shorter direct route.

D   This walk is ideal in fine weather, as it takes you to the shore of a lake, at a spot convenient for swimming. Children will want to enjoy themselves in the adventure playground nearby. From there you continue to Starling Cottage, which draws people from around the world to visit the home, from 1920 to 1927, of the poet Barbara Cottam.

E   If you want an easy, undemanding walk over flat ground, this walk will suit you perfectly. It passes the entrance to the famous Butter Caves visitor attraction, so you can combine a visit there with the walk, or just take shelter if it starts raining! On the final stage of the walk you pass through Wimpole, the village where Richard Merton, the architect of a number of local buildings, lived for much of his life.

Questions 1–5

The text on page 60 has five paragraphs, **A–E**.

Which paragraph mentions the following?

*Write the correct letter, **A–E**, in boxes 1–5 on your answer sheet.*

NB *You may use any letter more than once.*

1   the chance to go into caves

2   the chance to spend time beside a lake

3   some unusual architecture

4   unsuitability for young children

5   the length of the walk depending on the weather

Read the text below and answer Questions 6–14.

The Maplehampton scarecrow competition – a great success!

There was once a time when farmers all over the country put scarecrows in fields of growing crops. A traditional scarecrow was a model – usually life-size – of a man or woman dressed in old clothes, and their purpose was to frighten the birds away; though how successful they were is a matter of opinion!

Maplehampton's scarecrow competition took place on September 12th. Local farmers supplied everything needed to make a scarecrow – like pieces of wood to form a frame, and straw to stuff the scarecrow. The scarecrows were dressed in old clothes which the competitors brought with them.

The festival was held in the village hall, instead of outdoors as planned, due to the unusually high temperature. There were two classes, one for adults and one for children, all of them working in small teams. Over 20 teams took part, each creating one scarecrow. They were encouraged by an audience of around 50, and had ideas and guidance from local artist Tracey Sanzo.

The scarecrows were judged by a team of people from the village. The winning children's team made a scarecrow that looked like a giant bird – which would surely keep every real bird away! The winning adult team's scarecrow was dressed as an alien from another planet, and its face was painted to make it look very frightening – at least to human beings!

After the judging, many of the participants and the spectators had a picnic which they had brought. Some of the scarecrows then went home to their creators' gardens. Alice Cameron, a local farmer, liked one of the scarecrows so much, she bought it to stand on her balcony: she said she didn't need it to scare birds away from her crops, as only bird-scarers that made a noise were effective. She just wanted to be able to see it!

The event raised over £300 for village funds.

Questions 6–14

Do the following statements agree with the information given in the text on page 62?

In boxes 6–14 on your answer sheet, write

> **TRUE**   *if the statement agrees with the information*
> **FALSE**   *if the statement contradicts the information*
> **NOT GIVEN** *if there is no information on this*

6   Traditionally, most scarecrows were the same size as a human being.

7   The competition in September was the first one in Maplehampton.

8   The farmers who provided materials could take part in the competition.

9   Old clothes were supplied to the people who made the scarecrows.

10   The venue for the competition was changed because of the weather.

11   Competitors could get advice on making their scarecrows.

12   In the judges' opinion, the scarecrow dressed as an alien was better than the giant bird.

13   The competition organisers supplied a picnic for the competitors and spectators.

14   Alice Cameron bought a scarecrow to frighten birds away from her crops.

→ ◐ p. 126

SECTION 2   *Questions 15–27*

Read the text below and answer Questions 15–22.

Qualities that make a great barista

How to become a great maker and server of espresso-based coffee drinks

Truly great baristas take the time to develop the key skills that will enable them to deliver the highest possible quality of coffee-based beverage and service. As a barista, you must make a concerted effort to listen to your clientele and make sure the drinks you produce are correct in all respects. This is particularly important when you consider the sheer range and complexity of modern coffee drinks, which may start from a single (or double) shot of espresso but can include many additional elements. If you become distracted by the conversation that is going on nearby, you may ultimately miss the mark from a service perspective.

One thing that separates a great from a good barista is that the former is constantly busy and has a strong work ethic. You will often catch a great barista rinsing out the filter in their machines, for example, as this erodes the build-up of burnt coffee oil that can begin to impact on the quality and taste of each espresso shot. Similarly, do not be surprised to hear the sound of the coffee grinder at work. This highlights the keen attention to detail that distinguishes skilled baristas, as they have the desire and the awareness to make every drink with completely fresh ground coffee. This type of attentiveness helps baristas to get the most from the coffee that they use, as many of the delicate aromas found in espresso are lost when exposed to the open air.

Timing is everything when it comes to producing the perfect cup of coffee. A great barista knows precisely when to finish the extraction of espresso, at the point when the balance of flavour has reached its optimum levels. They also understand how important this is; those who act too soon are left with a drink without flavour while those who delay the finish risk burning the beverage and tainting it with a bitter after-taste.

When it comes to customer service, there is so much more to a coffee shop experience than drinking perfectly roasted blends. The atmosphere and the ambience also play a central role, and the interaction that the customer has with their barista sets the tone for an enjoyable experience. Great baristas ask their customers how their day is going or what they're going to do later; they read local newspapers and keep up with issues that really matter, all of which make a real difference in a competitive marketplace.

Questions 15–22

Complete the notes below.

*Choose **ONE WORD ONLY** from the text on page 64 for each answer.*

Write your answers in boxes 15–22 on your answer sheet.

Notes on being a great barista

Serving the customer

- Be sure you make drinks that are **15** .... for the customer

- Ignore any **16** .... around you

Using the equipment

- Clean the machine **17** .... regularly

- Grinding

  – always use ground coffee that is **18** ....

  – remember that air causes the smell to fade

Making the coffee

- Know when to stop making the espresso

  – too early reduces the **19** ....

  – too late makes the coffee **20** ....

Giving good customer service

- Talk to your customers

  – ask about the customers' **21** ....

  – know something about the important **22** .... in the area

---

Read the text below and answer Questions 23–27.

Running a meeting

If you're running a meeting for the first time, here are a few tips to help you

Prior to the meeting, think about the seating and arrange it in an appropriate way. A circle can work well for informal meetings, but sometimes the furniture cannot be re-arranged or rows are more suitable. Consider the participants and decide what is best. Before people arrive, it's a good idea to designate someone to stand at the entrance and greet everyone.

If the meeting is small, start by requesting everyone to introduce themselves and to give a bit of relevant information in addition to their name. This may be what they do or why they are there. For all meetings, you need to introduce the chairperson, i.e., yourself, and any other outside speakers you have invited.

Next, make sure everyone can see the agenda or has a copy of it. Briefly run through the items then take one point at a time, and make sure the group doesn't stray from that point until it has been dealt with. Encourage participation at all times so that attendees can contribute but don't let everyone talk at the same time. Try to keep discussions positive, but don't ignore conflicts – find a solution for them and make sure they are resolved before they grow.

Summarise points regularly and make clear action points. Write these down and don't forget to note who's doing what, and by when. Encourage everyone to feel able to volunteer for tasks and roles. It can help if the more experienced members of the group offer to share skills and knowledge, but don't let the same people take on all the work as this can lead to tension within the group.

At the end, remember to thank everyone for turning up and contributing. It can be nice to follow the meeting with a social activity like sharing a meal or going to a café.

Questions 23–27

Complete the flow chart below.

Choose **NO MORE THAN TWO WORDS** *from the text on page 66 for each answer.*

Write your answers in boxes 23–27 on your answer sheet.

Tips for running a meeting

Arrange seats according to the type of meeting and participants

⬇

In small meetings, ask people for some **23** ....
as they introduce themselves

⬇

Make sure the **24** ....
is available to everyone

⬇

Involve people in the discussion and solve
any **25** .... quickly if they arise

⬇

Note action points and who is responsible for them

⬇

Avoid **26** .... by involving a range of
people in tasks

⬇

Thank people for coming, and possibly have some kind of
27 .... afterwards

→ 🛇 p. 126

SECTION 3   *Questions 28–40*

Read the text on pages 69 and 70 and answer Questions 28–40.

Questions 28–33

The text on pages 69 and 70 has six sections, **A–F**.

Choose the correct heading for each section from the list of headings below.

*Write the correct number, **i–viii**, in boxes 28–33 on your answer sheet.*

List of Headings

   i The link between feathers and a wider international awareness

  ii An unsuitable decoration for military purposes

 iii A significant rise in the popularity of feathers

 iv Growing disapproval of the trapping of birds for their feathers

  v A new approach to researching the past

 vi Feathers as protection and as a symbol of sophistication

 vii An interesting relationship between the wearing of feathers and gender

viii A reason for the continued use of feathers by soldiers

---

28   Section **A**

29   Section **B**

30   Section **C**

31   Section **D**

32   Section **E**

33   Section **F**

Feathers as decoration in European history

A Today, we do not generally associate feathers with the military in Europe, yet history shows that in fact feathers have played an intriguing role in European military clothing. The Bersaglieri of the Italian Army, for example, still wear a bunch of long black feathers in their hats hanging down to one side, while British fusiliers have a clipped feather plume whose colour varies according to their regiment. The Royalists in the English Civil War adorned their headgear with ostrich feathers. 'Historically, feathers were an incredibly expressive accessory for men,' observes Cambridge historian, Professor Ulinka Rublack. 'Nobody has really looked at why this was the case. That's a story that I want to tell.'

Rublack is beginning to study the use of featherwork in early modern fashion as part of a joint project between the Universities of Cambridge, Basel and Bern. To the outsider, its preoccupations (her co-researchers are studying gold, glass and veils) might seem surprising. Yet such materials sustained significant economies and expertise.

B Rublack has spotted that something unusual started to happen with feathers during the 16th century. In 1500, they were barely worn at all in Europe; 100 years later they had become an indispensable accessory for the fashionable European man. In prosperous trading centres, the citizens started wearing hats bedecked with feathers from cranes and swallows. Headgear was specially manufactured so that feathers could be inserted more easily. By 1573, Plantin's Flemish–French dictionary was even obliged to offer words to describe people who chose not to wear them, recommending such terms as: 'the featherless' and 'unfeathered'.

Featherworking became big business. From Prague and Nuremberg to Paris and Madrid, people started to make a living from decorating feathers for clothing. Impressive efforts went into dyeing them. A 1548 recipe recommends using ashes, lead monoxide and river water to create a 'very beautiful' black, for example.

C Why this happened will become clearer as Rublack's project develops. One crucial driver, however, was exploration – the discovery of new lands, especially in South America. Compared with many of the other species that early European colonists encountered, exotic birds could be captured, transported and kept with relative ease. Europe experienced a sudden 'bird-craze', as exotic birds became a relatively common sight in the continent's largest markets.

Given the link with new territories and conquest, ruling elites wore feathers partly to express their power and reach. But there were also more complex reasons. In 1599, for example, Duke Frederick of Württemberg held a display at his court at which he personally appeared wearing a costume covered in exotic feathers and representing the Americas. This was not just a symbol of power, but of cultural connectedness, Rublack suggests: 'The message seems to be that he was embracing the global in a duchy that was quite insular and territorial.'

D Nor were feathers worn by the powerful alone. In 1530, a legislative assembly at Augsburg imposed restrictions on peasants and traders adopting what it clearly felt should be an elite fashion. The measure did not last, perhaps because health manuals of the era recommended feathers could keep the wearer safe from 'bad' air – cold, miasma, damp or excessive heat – all of which were regarded as hazardous. During the 1550s, Eleanor of Toledo had hats made from peacock feathers to keep her dry in the rain. Gradually, feathers came to indicate that the wearer was healthy and civilised. Artists and musicians took to wearing them as a mark of subtlety and style.

E As with most fads, this enthusiasm eventually wore off. By the mid-17th century, feathers were out of style, with one striking exception. Within the armies of Europe feathers remained an essential part of military costume.

Rublack thinks that there may have been several reasons for this strange contradiction. 'It's associated with the notion of graceful warfaring,' she says. 'This was a period when there were no standing armies and it was hard to draft soldiers. One solution was to aestheticise the military, to make it seem graceful and powerful.' Feathers became associated with the idea of an art of warfare.

They were also already a part of military garb among many native American peoples and in the Ottoman empire. Rublack believes that just as some of these cultures considered the feathers of certain birds to be highly significant, and sometimes sacred, European soldiers saw the feathers as imparting noble passions, bravery and courage.

F In time, her research may therefore reveal a tension about the ongoing use of feathers in this unlikely context. But, as she also notes, she is perhaps the first historian to have spotted the curious emotional resonance of feathers in military fashion at all. All this shows a sea-change in methodologies: historians now chart the ways in which our identities are shaped through deep connections with 'stuff' – the material objects that are parts of our lives.

Questions 34–36

*Choose the correct letter, **A**, **B**, **C** or **D**.*

Write the correct letter in boxes 34–36 on your answer sheet.

34 In Section B, what information is given about the use of feathers in the
16th century?

  A   Some were not real feathers, but imitations.
  B   They were sometimes coloured artificially.
  C   Birds were specially bred for their feathers.
  D   There was some disapproval of their use for decoration.

35 Rublack suggests the feather costume worn by Duke Frederick in 1599 represented

  A   a lack of sensitivity to American traditions.
  B   a rejection of the beliefs held by those around him.
  C   a positive attitude towards the culture of the Americas.
  D   a wish to follow a fashion of the time.

36 According to Rublack, one reason why feathers survived in European military
costume was because

  A   birds were seen as having religious significance.
  B   feathers suggested certain qualities about military activities.
  C   the power of feathers was feared by other cultures.
  D   soldiers came to associate particular birds with warlike qualities.

Questions 37–40

*Complete each sentence with the correct ending, **A–G**, below.*

*Write the correct letter, **A–G**, in boxes 37–40 on your answer sheet.*

37 Hats decorated with long black feathers

38 Feathers from cranes and swallows

39 Feathers from exotic birds

40 Peacock feathers

A	lost popularity in the 16th century.
B	were used as protection from bad weather.
C	are worn today by some soldiers.
D	could only be worn by men of noble birth.
E	were used to create an outfit worn by a person of high status.
F	were once awarded for military achievements.
G	became popular decorations for urban dwellers in the 16th century.

WRITING TASK 1

You should spend about 20 minutes on this task.

> *A magazine wants to include contributions from its readers for an article called 'The book that influenced me most'.*
>
> *Write a letter to the editor of the magazine about the book that influenced you most. In your letter*
> - *describe what this book was about*
> - *explain how this book influenced you*
> - *say whether this book would be likely to influence other people*

Write at least 150 words.

You do **NOT** need to write any addresses.

Begin your letter as follows:

Dear Sir or Madam,

WRITING TASK 2

You should spend about 40 minutes on this task.

Write about the following topic:

> **Some people spend most of their lives living close to where they were born.**
>
> **What might be the reasons for this?**
>
> **What are the advantages and disadvantages?**

Give reasons for your answer and include any relevant examples from your own knowledge or experience.

Write at least 250 words.

SPEAKING

PART 1

The examiner asks you about yourself, your home, work or studies and other familiar topics.

EXAMPLE

Summer

- Is summer your favourite time of year? [Why/Why not?]
- What do you do in summer when the weather's very hot? [Why?]
- Do you go on holiday every summer? [Why/Why not?]
- Did you enjoy the summer holidays when you were at school? [Why/Why not?]

PART 2

Describe a luxury item you would like to own in the future.

You should say:
   what item you would like to own
   what this item looks like
   why you would like to own this item

and explain whether you think you will ever own this item.

You will have to talk about the topic for one to two minutes. You have one minute to think about what you are going to say. You can make some notes to help you if you wish.

PART 3

Discussion topics:

Expensive items

Example questions:
Which expensive items would many young people (in your country) like to buy?
How do the expensive items that younger people want to buy differ from those that older people want to buy?
Do you think that people are more likely to buy expensive items for their friends or for themselves?

Rich people

Example questions:
How difficult is it to become very rich in today's world?
Do you agree that money does not necessarily bring happiness?
In what ways might rich people use their money to help society?

Test 4

PART 1   Questions 1–10

Complete the notes below.

Write ONE WORD AND/OR A NUMBER for each answer.

Listening test audio

Holiday rental

Owners' names: Jack Fitzgerald and Shirley Fitzgerald

Granary Cottage
- available for week beginning **1** .... May
- cost for the week: **2** £ ....

3 .... **Cottage**
- cost for the week: £480
- building was originally a **4** ....
- walk through doors from living room into a **5** ....
- several **6** .... spaces at the front
- bathroom has a shower
- central heating and stove that burns **7** ....
- views of old **8** .... from living room
- view of hilltop **9** .... from the bedroom

Payment
- deposit: £144
- deadline for final payment: end of **10** ....

PART 2   *Questions 11–20*

Listening test audio

Questions 11–14

*Choose the correct letter, **A**, **B** or **C**.*

Local council report on traffic and highways

11   A survey found people's main concern about traffic in the area was

    A   cuts to public transport.
    B   poor maintenance of roads.
    C   changes in the type of traffic.

12   Which change will shortly be made to the cycle path next to the river?

    A   It will be widened.
    B   It will be extended.
    C   It will be resurfaced.

13   Plans for a pedestrian crossing have been postponed because

    A   the Post Office has moved.
    B   the proposed location is unsafe.
    C   funding is not available at present.

14   On Station Road, notices have been erected

    A   telling cyclists not to leave their bikes outside the station ticket office.
    B   asking motorists to switch off engines when waiting at the level crossing.
    C   warning pedestrians to leave enough time when crossing the railway line.

Questions 15–20

Label the map below.

Write the correct letter, **A–I**, next to Questions 15–20.

Recreation ground after proposed changes

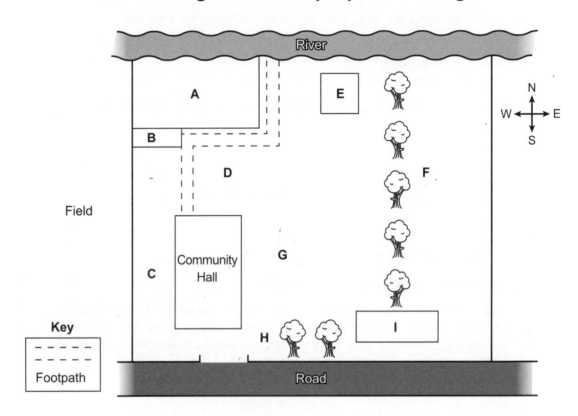

15 New car park   ....

16 New cricket pitch   ....

17 Children's playground ....

18 Skateboard ramp   ....

19 Pavilion   ....

20 Notice board   ....

PART 3   *Questions 21–30*

Listening test audio

Questions 21–22

*Choose **TWO** letters, **A–E**.*

Which **TWO** benefits of city bike-sharing schemes do the students agree are the most important?

    A   reducing noise pollution
    B   reducing traffic congestion
    C   improving air quality
    D   encouraging health and fitness
    E   making cycling affordable

Questions 23–24

*Choose **TWO** letters, **A–E**.*

Which **TWO** things do the students think are necessary for successful bike-sharing schemes?

    A   Bikes should have a GPS system.
    B   The app should be easy to use.
    C   Public awareness should be raised.
    D   Only one scheme should be available.
    E   There should be a large network of cycle lanes.

Questions 25–30

What is the speakers' opinion of the bike-sharing schemes in each of the following cities?

*Choose **SIX** answers from the box and write the correct letter, **A–G**, next to Questions 25–30.*

Opinion of bike-sharing scheme

A   They agree it has been disappointing.

B   They think it should be cheaper.

C   They are surprised it has been so successful.

D   They agree that more investment is required.

E   They think the system has been well designed.

F   They disagree about the reasons for its success.

G   They think it has expanded too quickly.

Cities

25   Amsterdam   ....

26   Dublin   ....

27   London   ....

28   Buenos Aires   ....

29   New York   ....

30   Sydney   ....

PART 4 · *Questions 31–40*

Complete the notes below.

Write ONE WORD ONLY for each answer.

Listening test audio

THE EXTINCTION OF THE DODO BIRD

The dodo was a large flightless bird which used to inhabit the island of Mauritius.

History

- 1507 – Portuguese ships transporting **31** .... stopped at the island to collect food and water.
- 1638 – The Dutch established a **32** .... on the island.
- They killed the dodo birds for their meat.
- The last one was killed in 1681.

Description

- The only record we have is written descriptions and pictures (possibly unreliable).
- A Dutch painting suggests the dodo was very **33** ....
- The only remaining soft tissue is a dried **34** ....
- Recent studies of a dodo skeleton suggest the birds were capable of rapid

  35 ....
- It's thought they were able to use their small wings to maintain

  36 ....
- Their **37** .... was of average size.
- Their sense of **38** .... enabled them to find food.

Reasons for extinction

- Hunting was probably not the main cause.
- Sailors brought dogs and monkeys.
- **39** .... also escaped onto the island and ate the birds' eggs.
- The arrival of farming meant the **40** .... was destroyed.

→ p. 127 p. 119

READING

SECTION 1   *Questions 1–14*

Read the text below and answer Questions 1–8.

The best hiking boots

Whether you're climbing a mountain or walking in the country, be sure to buy the right boots, writes Sian Lewis

A   Hanwag Tatra Boots

These boots are expensive but will give you a lifetime of wear. They are a wide fit and offer excellent ankle support. They passed our waterproof test when worn on long, rainy walks, although they are a bit heavy.

B   Scarpa Peak Gore-tex Boots

These are good all-round boots that have kept our feet dry in heavy rain, snow and mud. They are warm and comfortable to wear straight out of the box and continue to be so even after many kilometres. A great choice for all seasons.

C   Keen Terradora Ethos

These are meant for spring and summer walks and for putting in your backpack for treks in hot climates. They will never weigh you down. Their soles grip well and despite not being waterproof, they are quick-drying when they get wet.

D   Danner Jag

Danner's retro boots are one of the heavier ones we reviewed. They take a week or two for your feet to get used to them, but we found them waterproof even in heavy rain. These are boots for the style conscious, but still suitable for demanding walks.

E   Merrell Siren Sport Q2 Mid Boots

We've worn these boots in freezing cold conditions and our feet felt comfortable. Remember to pull the laces firmly when you put these boots on as they are rather wide around the ankles.

F   Teva Arrowood Mid WP

The soft leather might not be tough enough for extreme environments, but these boots get top marks for comfort. They're waterproof, but we found this wore off after about 20 wet walks. You can, however, get round this problem by using a protective spray on them.

G   Regatta Clydebank Mid Boots

These boots are reasonably priced and they performed well in heavy rain. They don't grip the ground as well as some other boots and aren't very warm in cold winter weather so we'd say they're best for country walks in spring and summer.

Questions 1–8

*Look at the seven reviews of hiking boots, **A–G**, on page 82.*

For which hiking boots are the following statements true?

*Write the correct letter, **A–G**, in boxes 1–8 on your answer sheet.*

***NB** You may use any letter more than once.*

1 These boots are a good choice for people who want to look smart when they are walking.

2 People do not need to spend time getting their feet accustomed to these boots.

3 These boots should last for many years.

4 People find these boots useful when travelling as they are not heavy.

5 One feature of these boots does not continue to be effective for very long.

6 These boots do not keep the rain out.

7 It is important to make sure these boots are done up tightly before starting a walk.

8 These boots should suit people who don't want to spend a lot.

Read the text below and answer Questions 9–14.

Beekeeping workshop at Elm Farm

If you've ever wanted to keep bees and have your own delicious honey, there's no better time to begin!

Whether you're keen to learn everything you need to know to get you started, or simply extremely interested in the idea of keeping bees, this one-day interactive workshop will teach you the fascinating secrets of the honeybee and how to care for and keep bees.

Our day begins here on the farm, getting to know about the honeybee, specifically the kind we keep here, and their fascinating history. You will find out about and try for yourself the equipment beekeepers use to care for their bees and discover the many different types of hives bee colonies live in and their different uses. You'll learn about the life cycle of a colony, disease prevention and caring for bees and of course how to harvest honey for your personal use or for sale.

Then it's time to try on your bee suit and meet our bees. We'll teach you how to open the hive, recognise the different bees in it (including how to spot the queen!) and explain what they're doing in different parts of the hive.

What's included in the price?

We'll provide everything you need, including unlimited organic tea or coffee, lunch cooked in our outdoor, wood-fired oven and beekeeping suits for the day. Just bring a pair of thick boots with you. You'll leave with plenty of notes and resources, including a packet of bee-friendly wildflower seeds and, courtesy of BJ Sherriff, the leading supplier of beekeeping clothing, an exclusive 25% discount for anything in their online store.

We like to run our workshops fairly and honestly. Your booking secures a very limited place, so is non-refundable – if you can't make it, you can send a friend or colleague instead though. If at the end of any of our workshops, you don't believe that it has helped you to achieve what it set out to, we will gladly provide a full refund.

Places are strictly limited so please do book early to avoid disappointment.

Questions 9–14

Do the following statements agree with the information given in the text on page 84?

In boxes 9–14 on your answer sheet, write

TRUE   *if the statement agrees with the information*
FALSE   *if the statement contradicts the information*
NOT GIVEN   *if there is no information on this*

9   The workshop is only suitable for people who already keep their own bees.

10   Participants will meet people who are involved in selling honey to the public.

11   Vegetarian refreshments are available if requested in advance.

12   Participants will need to pay extra to hire appropriate clothes for the workshop.

13   Protective footwear will be required during the workshop.

14   If someone has to cancel before the workshop, the fee will be repaid.

→ ❍ p. 128

SECTION 2   *Questions 15–27*

Read the text below and answer Questions 15–20.

Should you pay someone to write your CV?

In my view, the belief that the individual is the best person to write their own CV is not always true. Although many people can write their own CVs, and do it well, others struggle with a variety of problems initially, such as not knowing how to structure a CV or how to highlight their most relevant strengths.

Through in-depth consultation, a professional CV writer can help identify exactly what is necessary for a particular role, cut out unnecessary or irrelevant details, and pinpoint what makes the individual stand out. This level of objectivity is one of the major benefits of working with a professional writer. It's often difficult to stand back from your own career history to assess what's relevant or not, or to choose the most appropriate qualities.

If you do choose to work with a professional CV writer, here are some tips:

Ask for a CV writer who has experience in your sector. HR professionals and recruiters with relevant experience can also have valuable insights into what companies are looking for.

Look for someone who's prepared to take the time to find out your core qualities, who can choose exactly the right words for maximum impact and who understands what and where to edit. Ask to see samples of their work or use personal recommendations before you choose a CV writing service.

You'll probably need to answer an in-depth email questionnaire or be interviewed before any writing actually starts. The more you can give your CV writer to work with, the better, so the promise of a quick turnaround time isn't always going to result in the best possible CV. Take the time to think about and jot down your career aims, your past successes, and the value you bring, before you start the whole process. Your CV will probably be used as a springboard for questions at interview, so you need to make sure you feel happy with the way it's being written and with the choice of words. Being involved in the writing process means your CV sounds authentic.

Questions 15–20

Complete the sentences below.

Choose ONE WORD ONLY from the text on page 86 for each answer.

Write your answers in boxes 15–20 on your answer sheet.

15 Some jobseekers have difficulty with their CV because they have not learnt which qualities they should ....

16 Professional CV writers know which .... are best left out of the CV.

17 CV writers with knowledge of a particular field of work often provide useful .... about the skills firms expect from job applicants.

18 It is advisable to request .... of what a professional CV writer has previously produced.

19 Professional CV writers often ask jobseekers to work through a .... as a first step.

20 If the jobseeker assists the professional writer, the tone of the CV will be ....

Read the text below and answer Questions 21–27.

Starting a new job

First impressions really do last, so it's important you perform well on your first day in the new job. Here are our top tips that will help you sail through your first day with ease.

A new job is a great opportunity to hit the reset button. If you got into the habit of skipping breakfast at your last job, fit it in now or experiment with getting a workout in before going to the office. Having a routine you like and sticking to it definitely impacts on your overall happiness.

You've probably already been into the office for an interview, so you'll have some idea of what the dress code is. While you definitely want to feel comfortable, it's best to play it safe, leaning towards a smarter and more polished look on your first day.

You don't want to be late, but getting to the office way too early can also potentially upset not only your schedule but other people's too. A good rule of thumb is to try and arrive 15 minutes ahead of the agreed start time.

Accepting an invite to lunch with your boss and co-workers will allow you to get to know the people you'll be working with on a more personal level. It will also help you get a handle on personalities and work styles. To ensure the lunch goes well, have a few conversation starters in mind. That way, if the talk dries up, you can get it going again.

One of the big outcomes of going through a job search is you learn loads about yourself. In particular, you learn what you want and don't want, and what skills you bring to the table. With this new-found understanding, take some time over the initial period to think about what goals you have for your new role. In identifying these early on, you'll be one step closer to positioning yourself for success.

It's important that you approach your new job with an open mind, and that you're ready to soak it all in. Be patient with yourself as you figure out how you fit in, and make sure you understand the way things are done before rushing into giving suggestions on improvements.

Remember they hired you for a reason, so smile, relax a little and enjoy the first day of your next big thing.

Questions 21–27

Complete the notes below.

*Choose **NO MORE THAN TWO WORDS** from the text on page 88 for each answer.*

Write your answers in boxes 21–27 on your answer sheet.

How best to tackle a new job

The first day

- Before arriving at work

  - try out a different morning **21** .... that will create a sense of well-being.

  - make sure your chosen outfit conforms to the company's **22** ....

- If you eat with colleagues at midday:

  - it will provide information on their **23** .... and the way they operate.

  - it may be wise to prepare some **24** .... to help the interaction flow.

During the first few weeks

- work out some **25** .... and how to go about fulfilling them.

- try to keep a completely **26** .... as you settle into the post.

- avoid making proposals for **27** .... too soon.

SECTION 3   *Questions 28–40*

Read the text below and answer Questions 28–40.

History of women's football in Britain

Women's football in Britain has deeper roots than might be expected. In one town in 18th-century Scotland, single women played an annual match against their married counterparts, though the motives behind the contest were not purely sporting. Some accounts say that the games were watched by a crowd of single men, who hoped to pick out a potential bride based on her footballing ability.

By the late 19th century, with the men's game spreading across Britain like wildfire, women also began to take up association football. Early pioneers included Nettie J Honeyball, who founded the British Ladies' Football Club (BLFC) in 1895. Honeyball was an alias: like many of the middle- and upper-class women who played in the late 19th century, she was not keen to publicise her involvement with a contact sport played on muddy fields. We know more about Lady Florence Dixie, who was appointed president of the BLFC in 1895 and who was an ardent believer in equality between the sexes.

The BLFC arranged games between teams representing the north and the south of England, where money would be raised for those in need. These initially attracted healthy numbers of supporters although early newspaper reports were not particularly generous, with one reporter suggesting 'when the novelty has worn off, I do not think women's football will attract the crowds'. And crowds did drop off as the growing popularity of the men's game came to dominate public interest. In a country where women were not yet allowed to vote, it would take extraordinary circumstances for their efforts on the football pitch to attract widespread attention.

Those circumstances arose in 1914 with the outbreak of the First World War. With many men leaving their jobs to join the army, women started to work in factories and just as men had done before them, they began to play informal games of football during their lunch breaks. After some initial uncertainty, their superiors came to see these games as a means to boost morale and thus increase productivity. Teams soon formed and friendly matches were arranged.

In the town of Preston in the north of England, the female workers at a manufacturing company called Dick, Kerr & Co showed a particular aptitude for the game. Watching from a window above the yard where they played, office worker Alfred Frankland spotted their talent and he set about forming a team. Under Frankland's management, they soon drew significant crowds to see their games. Known as Dick, Kerr's Ladies, they beat rival factory Arundel Coulthard 4–0 on Christmas Day 1917, with 10,000 watching at Preston stadium.

After the war ended in 1918 the Dick, Kerr's side and other women's teams continued to draw large crowds. In 1920 there were around 150 women's sides in England and Dick, Kerr's Ladies packed 53,000 into Everton's Goodison Park stadium. The same year, the team found their one true genius: Lily Parr. Parr grew up playing football with her brothers, and began her career with her town's ladies' team at the age of 14. When they played against the Dick, Kerr's side, she caught Frankland's eye and was offered a job at the factory – as well as a spot on the team. Close to six-feet tall and with jet-black hair, she had a ferocious appetite and a fierce left foot. She is credited with 43 goals during her first season playing for Dick, Kerr's Ladies and around 1,000 in total.

By 1921 Dick, Kerr's Ladies were regularly attracting crowds in the tens of thousands. But the year ended in catastrophe for the women's game. The Football Association (FA) – officially the governing body for the sport as a whole, but really only concerned with men's competitions – had always taken a poor view of female participation. Women's football was tolerated during the war, but in the years that followed, driven by the fear that the women's game could affect Football League attendances, the FA sought to assert itself.

Its solution was decisive and brutal. On 5 December 1921, the FA banned its members from allowing women's football to be played at its grounds, saying that football was 'quite unsuitable for females'. The FA also forbade its members from acting as referees at women's games. To all intents and purposes, women's football in England was outlawed.

The FA also suggested that an excessive proportion of the gate receipts were absorbed in expenses and an inadequate percentage devoted to charity. No such obligation to donate profits existed for men's clubs and no proof of financial mismanagement was presented, but there was little the women's clubs could do in response.

There was outrage from players, with the captain of Plymouth Ladies remarking that the FA was 'a hundred years behind the times' and calling its decision 'purely sex prejudice'.

It was not until 1966 that serious efforts to revive the women's game began, but progress remained painfully slow. It took pressure from the Union of European Football Associations (UEFA), to finally force the FA to end restrictions on women's football in 1971. By this time, half a century of progress had been lost.

Questions 28–31

Choose the correct letter, **A**, **B**, **C** or **D**.

Write the correct letter in boxes 28–31 on your answer sheet.

28 In the first paragraph, the writer says that in 18th-century Scotland

    A only unmarried women were allowed to play football.
    B women's football was more common than men's football.
    C women were sometimes forbidden to watch football matches.
    D skill at football might be considered when choosing a wife.

29 The writer says that Nettie J Honeyball was unwilling to

    A take an active part in team sports.
    B mix with people she considered lower class.
    C let the public know of her involvement in football.
    D take a leadership role in the British Ladies' Football Club.

30 The writer suggests that in Britain, between 1895 and 1914,

    A society was not yet ready for women's football.
    B there were false reports of the decline of women's football.
    C the media felt that women's football should not be allowed.
    D women's football mainly attracted people because it was unusual.

31 After the First World War broke out in 1914, factory managers

    A were initially unwilling to employ women.
    B played in matches against female employees.
    C allowed extra time for their employees to play football.
    D decided that women's football might have positive effects.

Questions 32–37

Look at the following statements (Questions 32–37) and the list of football organisations below.

*Match each statement with the correct organisation, **A**, **B**, **C** or **D**.*

*Write the correct letter, **A**, **B**, **C** or **D**, in boxes 32–37 on your answer sheet.*

NB *You may use any letter more than once.*

32 It felt threatened by the rise of women's football.

33 It was established by a male office worker.

34 It donated money from football matches to good causes.

35 It called for the ending of the ban on women's football in Britain.

36 It was accused of being old-fashioned.

37 It was led by a believer in women's rights.

List of Football Organisations

A   the British Ladies' Football Club (BLFC)

B   the Dick, Kerr's Ladies team

C   the Football Association (FA)

D   the Union of European Football Associations (UEFA)

Questions 38–40

Complete the summary below.

*Choose **ONE WORD ONLY** from the text on pages 90 and 91 for each answer.*

Write your answers in boxes 38–40 on your answer sheet.

A catastrophic year for women's football

At the end of 1921, women's football teams were forbidden to use the

38 .... of the Football Association, and were not allowed to have

Football Association members as **39** .... The FA said that women's

clubs did not give enough to charity, and that there had been mismanagement of funds.

Female workers accused the FA of **40** .... against women, but the

ban continued until 1971.

WRITING TASK 1

You should spend about 20 minutes on this task.

> *Your friend has been offered a place on a course at the university where you studied. He/She would like your advice about finding a place to live.*
>
> *Write an email to your friend. In your email*
> - *describe where you lived when you were a student at the university*
> - *recommend the best way for him/her to look for accommodation*
> - *warn him/her of mistakes students make when choosing accommodation*

Write at least 150 words.

You do **NOT** need to write any addresses.

Begin your email as follows:

Dear .... *,*

WRITING TASK 2

You should spend about 40 minutes on this task.

Write about the following topic:

> **Some people say that now is the best time in history to be living.**
>
> **What is your opinion about this?**
>
> **What other time in history would be interesting to live in?**

Give reasons for your answer and include any relevant examples from your own knowledge or experience.

Write at least 250 words.

SPEAKING

PART 1

The examiner asks you about yourself, your home, work or studies and other familiar topics.

EXAMPLE

Fast food

- What kinds of fast food have you tried? [Why/Why not?]
- Do you ever use a microwave to cook food quickly? [Why/Why not?]
- How popular are fast food restaurants where you live? [Why/Why not?]
- When would you go to a fast-food restaurant? [Why/Why not?]

PART 2

> **Describe some technology (e.g. an app, phone, software program) that you decided to stop using.**
>
> **You should say:**
> **when and where you got this technology**
> **why you started using this technology**
> **why you decided to stop using it**
>
> **and explain how you feel about the decision you made.**

You will have to talk about the topic for one to two minutes. You have one minute to think about what you are going to say. You can make some notes to help you if you wish.

PART 3

Discussion topics:

Computer games

Example questions:
What kinds of computer games do people play in your country?
Why do people enjoy playing computer games?
Do you think that all computer games should have a minimum age for players?

Technology in the classroom

Example questions:
In what ways can technology in the classroom be helpful?
Do you agree that students are often better at using technology than their teachers?
Do you believe that computers will ever replace human teachers?

Audioscripts

TEST 1

PART 1

SARAH:	Hello. Children's Engineering Workshops.
FATHER:	Oh hello. I wanted some information about the workshops in the school holidays.
SARAH:	Sure.
FATHER:	I have two daughters who are interested. The younger one's Lydia, she's four – do you take children as young as that?
SARAH:	Yes, our Tiny Engineers workshop is for four to five-year-olds.
FATHER:	What sorts of activities do they do?
SARAH:	All sorts. For example, they work together to design a special cover that goes round an egg, so that when it's inside they can drop it from a height and it doesn't break. Well, sometimes it does break but that's part of the fun! *Q1*
FATHER:	Right. And Lydia loves building things. Is there any opportunity for her to do that?
SARAH:	Well, they have a competition to see who can make the highest tower. You'd be amazed how high they can go. *Q2*
FATHER:	Right.
SARAH:	But they're learning all the time as well as having fun. For example, one thing they do is to design and build a car that's attached to a balloon, and the force of the air in that actually powers the car and makes it move along. They go really fast too. *Q3*
SARAH:	OK, well, all this sounds perfect.

FATHER:	Now Carly, that's my older daughter, has just had her seventh birthday, so presumably she'd be in a different group?
SARAH:	Yes, she'd be in the Junior Engineers. That's for children from six to eight.
FATHER:	And do they do the same sorts of activities?
SARAH:	Some are the same, but a bit more advanced. So they work out how to build model vehicles, things like cars and trucks, but also how to construct animals using the same sorts of material and technique, and then they learn how they can program them and make them move. *Q4*
FATHER:	So they learn a bit of coding?
SARAH:	They do. They pick it up really quickly. We're there to help if they need it, but they learn from one another too.
FATHER:	Right. And do they have competitions too?
SARAH:	Yes, with the Junior Engineers, it's to use recycled materials like card and wood to build a bridge, and the longest one gets a prize. *Q5*
FATHER:	That sounds fun. I wouldn't mind doing that myself!
SARAH:	Then they have something a bit different, which is to think up an idea for a five-minute movie and then film it, using special animation software. You'd be amazed what they come up with. *Q6*
FATHER:	And of course, that's something they can put on their phone and take home to show all their friends.
SARAH:	Exactly. And then they also build a robot in the shape of a human, and they decorate it and program it so that it can move its arms and legs. *Q7*

FATHER:	Perfect. So, is it the same price as the Tiny Engineers?
SARAH:	It's just a bit more: £50 for the five weeks.
FATHER:	And are the classes on a Monday?
SARAH:	They used to be, but we found it didn't give our staff enough time to clear up after the first workshop, so we moved them to <u>Wednesdays</u>. The classes are held in the morning from ten to eleven.
FATHER:	OK. That's better for me actually. And what about the location? Where exactly are the workshops held?
SARAH:	They're in building 10A – there's a big sign on the door, you can't miss it, and that's in <u>Fradstone</u> Industrial Estate.
FATHER:	Sorry?
SARAH:	Fradstone – that's F-R-A-D-S-T-O-N-E.
FATHER:	And that's in Grasford, isn't it?
SARAH:	Yes, up past the station.
FATHER:	And will I have any <u>parking</u> problems there?
SARAH:	No, there's always plenty available. So would you like to enrol Lydia and Carly now?
FATHER:	OK.
SARAH:	So can I have your full name …

Q8

Q9

Q10

PART 2

Good.morning, everyone, and welcome to Stevenson's, one of the country's major manufacturers of metal goods. Thank you for choosing us for your two weeks of work experience. My name is Julia Simmons, and since the beginning of this year I've been the managing director.

Stevenson's is quite an old company. Like me, the founder, Ronald Stevenson, went into the steel industry when he left school – that was in 1923. <u>He set up this company when he finished his apprenticeship, in 1926</u>, although he actually started making plans two years earlier, in 1924. He was a very determined young man!

Q11

Stevenson's long-term plan was to manufacture components for the machine tools industry – although in fact that never came about – and for the automotive industry, that is, cars and lorries. However, there was a delay of five years before that happened, because shortly before the company went into production, <u>Stevenson was given the opportunity to make goods for hospitals and other players in the healthcare industry, so that's what we did for the first five years</u>.

Q12

Over the years, we've expanded the premises considerably – we were lucky that the site is big enough, so <u>moving to a new location has never been necessary</u>. However, the layout is far from ideal for modern machinery and production methods, so <u>we intend to carry out major refurbishment of this site</u> over the next five years.

Q13

I'd better give you some idea of what you'll be doing during your two weeks with us, so you know what to expect. <u>Most mornings you'll have a presentation from one of the managers</u>, to learn about their department, starting this morning with research and development. And you'll all spend some time in each department, observing what's going on and talking to people – as long as you don't stop them from doing their work altogether! In the past, a teacher from your school has come in at the end of each week to find out how the group were getting on, but your school isn't able to arrange that this year.

Q14

OK, now I'll briefly help you to orientate yourselves around the site. As you can see, we're in the reception area, which we try to make attractive and welcoming to visitors. There's a

corridor running left from here, and if you go along that, the door facing you at the end is the   Q15
entrance to the coffee room. This looks out onto the main road on one side, and some trees
on the other, and that'll be where you meet each morning.

The factory is the very big room on the far side of the site. Next to it is the warehouse, which   Q16
can be accessed by lorries going up the road to the turning area at the end. You can get to
the warehouse by crossing to the far side of the courtyard, and then the door is on your right.

Somewhere you'll be keen to find is the staff canteen. This is right next to reception. I can   Q17
confidently say that the food's very good, but the view isn't. The windows on one side look
onto a corridor and courtyard, which aren't very attractive at all, and on the other onto the
access road, which isn't much better.

You'll be using the meeting room quite often, and you'll find it by walking along the corridor to   Q18
the left of the courtyard, and continuing along it to the end. The meeting room is the last one
on the right, and I'm afraid there's no natural daylight in the room.

Then you'll need to know where some of the offices are. The human resources department is   Q19
at the front of this building, so you head to the left along the corridor from reception, and it's
the second room you come to. It looks out onto the main road.

And finally, the boardroom, where you'll be meeting sometimes. That has quite a pleasant   Q20
view, as it looks out on to the trees. Go along the corridor past the courtyard, right to the end.
The boardroom is on the left, next to the factory.

OK, now are there any questions before we ...

PART 3

JESS:	How are you getting on with your art project, Tom?
TOM:	OK. Like, they gave us the theme of birds to base our project on, and I'm not really all that interested in wildlife. But I'm starting to get into it. I've pretty well finished the introductory stage.
JESS:	So have I. When they gave us all those handouts with details of books and websites to look at, I was really put off, but the more I read, the more interested I got.
TOM:	Me too. I found I could research so many different aspects of birds in art – colour, movement, texture. So I was looking forward to the Bird Park visit.
JESS:	What a letdown! It poured with rain and we hardly saw a single bird. Much less use than the trip to the Natural History Museum.
TOM:	Yeah. I liked all the stuff about evolution there. The workshop sessions with Dr Fletcher were good too, especially the brainstorming sessions.
JESS:	I missed those because I was ill. I wish we could've seen the projects last year's students did.
TOM:	Mm. I suppose they want us to do our own thing, not copy.
JESS:	Have you drafted your proposal yet?
TOM:	Yes, but I haven't handed it in. I need to amend some parts. I've realised the notes from my research are almost all just descriptions, I haven't actually evaluated anything. So I'll have to fix that.
JESS:	Oh, I didn't know we had to do that. I'll have to look at that too. Did you do a timeline for the project?
TOM:	Yes, and a mind map.
JESS:	Yeah, so did I. I quite enjoyed that. But it was hard having to explain the basis for my decisions in my action plan.

The Q21/Q22 markers appear beside the first JESS and second JESS lines; the Q23/Q24 marker appears beside the TOM line about evaluating.

TOM:	What?
JESS:	You know, give a rationale.
TOM:	I didn't realise we had to do that. OK, I can add it now. And I've done the video diary presentation, and worked out what I want my outcome to be in the project.
JESS:	Someone told me <u>it's best not to be too precise about your actual outcome</u> at this stage, so you have more scope to explore your ideas later on. <u>So I'm going to go back to my proposal to make it a bit more vague.</u>
TOM:	Really? <u>OK, I'll change that too then.</u>

Q23/Q24

TOM:	One part of the project I'm unsure about is where we choose some paintings of birds and say what they mean to us. Like, I chose a painting of <u>a falcon by Landseer.</u> I like it because the bird's standing there with his head turned to one side, but he seems to be staring straight at you. But I can't just say it's a bit scary, can I?
JESS:	<u>You could talk about the possible danger suggested by the bird's look.</u>
TOM:	Oh, <u>OK.</u>
JESS:	There's a picture of <u>a fish hawk by Audubon</u> I like. It's swooping over the water with a fish in its talons, and with great black wings which take up most of the picture.
TOM:	So you could discuss it in relation to predators and food chains?
JESS:	Well actually I think <u>I'll concentrate on the impression of rapid motion it gives.</u>
TOM:	Right.
JESS:	Do you know that picture of <u>a kingfisher by van Gogh</u> – it's perching on a reed growing near a stream.
TOM:	Yes it's got these beautiful blue and red and black shades.
JESS:	Mm hm. I've actually chosen it because <u>I saw a real kingfisher once when I was little, I was out walking with my grandfather</u>, and I've never forgotten it.
TOM:	So we can use a personal link?
JESS:	Sure.
TOM:	OK. There's <u>a portrait called *William Wells*</u>, I can't remember the artist but it's a middle-aged man who's just shot a bird. And his expression, and the way he's holding the bird in his hand suggests he's not sure about what he's done. To me <u>it's about how ambiguous people are in the way they exploit the natural world.</u>
JESS:	Interesting. There's <u>Gauguin's picture *Vairumati*.</u> He did it in Tahiti. It's a woman with a white bird behind her that is eating a lizard, and what I'm interested in is what idea this bird refers to. Apparently, <u>it's a reference to the never-ending cycle of existence.</u>
TOM:	Wow. I chose <u>a portrait of a little boy, Giovanni de Medici.</u> <u>He's holding a tiny bird in one fist.</u> I like the way <u>he's holding it carefully so he doesn't hurt it.</u>
JESS:	Ah right.

Q25, Q26, Q27, Q28, Q29, Q30

PART 4

Ancient philosophy is not just about talking or lecturing, or even reading long, dense books. In fact, it is something people have used throughout history – to solve their problems and to achieve their greatest triumphs.

Specifically, I am referring to Stoicism, which, in my opinion, is <u>the most practical of all philosophies</u> and therefore the most appealing. Stoicism was founded in Ancient Greece by Zeno of Citium in the early 3rd century BC, but was practised by the likes of Epictetus, Cato,

Q31

Seneca and Marcus Aurelius. Amazingly, we still have access to these ideas, despite the fact that <u>the most famous Stoics never wrote anything down for publication</u>. Cato definitely didn't. Marcus Aurelius never intended his *Meditations* to be anything but personal. Seneca's letters were, well, letters and Epictetus' thoughts come to us by way of a note-taking student.

Q32

Stoic principles were based on the idea that its followers could have an unshakable happiness in this life and the key to achieving this was virtue. The road to virtue, in turn, lay in understanding that destructive emotions, like anger and jealousy, are under our conscious control – they don't have to control us, because we can learn to control them. In the words of Epictetus: "<u>external events I cannot control, but the choices I make with regard to them, I do control</u>".

Q33

The modern day philosopher and writer Nassim Nicholas Taleb defines a Stoic as someone who has <u>a different perspective on experiences which most of us would see as wholly negative</u>; a Stoic "transforms fear into caution, pain into transformation, mistakes into initiation and desire into undertaking". Using this definition as a model, we can see that throughout the centuries Stoicism has been practised in more recent history by kings, presidents, artists, writers and entrepreneurs.

Q34

The founding fathers of the United States were inspired by the philosophy. George Washington was introduced to Stoicism by his neighbours at age seventeen, and later, <u>put on a play based on the life of Cato to inspire his men</u>. Thomas Jefferson kept a copy of Seneca beside his bed.

Q35

Writers and artists have also been inspired by the stoics. Eugène Delacroix, the renowned French Romantic artist (known best for his painting *Liberty Leading the People*) was an ardent Stoic, referring to it as his "consoling religion".

The economist <u>Adam Smith's theories on capitalism were significantly influenced by the Stoicism</u> that he studied as a schoolboy, under a teacher who had translated Marcus Aurelius' works.

Q36

Today's political leaders are no different, with many finding their inspiration from the ancient texts. Former US president Bill Clinton rereads Marcus Aurelius every single year, and many have compared former President Obama's calm leadership style to that of Cato. Wen Jiabao, the former prime minister of China, claims that *Meditations* is one of two books he travels with and that he has read it more than one hundred times over the course of his life.

Stoicism had a profound influence on Albert Ellis, who invented <u>Cognitive Behaviour Therapy</u>, which is used to help people manage their problems by changing the way that they think and behave. <u>It's most commonly used to treat depression.</u> The idea is that we can take control of our lives by <u>challenging the irrational beliefs that create our faulty thinking, symptoms and behaviours by using logic</u> instead.

Q37

Q38

Stoicism has also become popular in the world of business. Stoic principles can build the resilience and state of mind required to overcome setbacks because <u>Stoics teach turning obstacles into opportunity</u>. A lesson every business entrepreneur needs to learn.

Q39

I would argue that studying Stoicism is as relevant today as it was 2,000 years ago, thanks to its brilliant <u>insights into how to lead a good life</u>. At the very root of the thinking, there is a very

Q40

simple way of living – control what you can and accept what you can't. <u>This is not as easy as it sounds and will require considerable practice</u> – it can take a lifetime to master. The Stoics also believed the most important foundation for a good and happy life is not money, fame, power or pleasure, but having a disciplined and principled character – something which seems to resonate with many people today.

PART 1

EMPLOYEE:	Hello, Picturerep. Can I help you?
WOMAN:	Oh, hi. I saw your advertisement about copying pictures to disk and I'd like a bit more information about what you do.
EMPLOYEE:	Sure. What would you like to know?
WOMAN:	Well, I've got a box full of old family photos that's been up in the attic for years, some of them must be 50 or 60 years old, and I'd like to get them converted to digital format.
EMPLOYEE:	Sure, we can do that for you.
WOMAN:	Right. And what about size? The photos are all sorts of sizes – are there any restrictions?
EMPLOYEE:	Well the maximum size of photo we can do with our normal service is 30 centimetres. And each picture must be at least 4 centimetres, that's the minimum we can cope with.
WOMAN:	That should be fine. And some of them are in a <u>frame</u> – should I take them out before I send them?
EMPLOYEE:	Yes please, we can't copy them otherwise. And also the photos must all be separate, they mustn't be stuck into an album.
WOMAN:	OK, that's not a problem. So can you give me an idea of how much this will cost? I've got about 360 photos I think.
EMPLOYEE:	We charge <u>£195 for 300 to 400 photos</u> for the basic service.
WOMAN:	OK. And does that include the disk?
EMPLOYEE:	Yes, one disk – but you can get extra ones for £5 each.
WOMAN:	That's good. So do I need to pay when I send you the photos?
EMPLOYEE:	No, we won't need anything until we've actually copied the pictures. Then we'll let you know how much it is, and <u>once we've received the payment</u>, we'll send the parcel off to you.
WOMAN:	Right.

Q1

Q2

Q3

- -

EMPLOYEE:	Is there anything else you'd like to ask about our services?
WOMAN:	Yes. I've roughly sorted out the photos into groups, according to what they're about – so can you keep them in those groups when you copy them.
EMPLOYEE:	Sure. We'll save each group in a different folder on the disk and if you like, you can suggest a name for each folder –
WOMAN:	So I could have one called <u>'Grandparents'</u> for instance?
EMPLOYEE:	Exactly.
WOMAN:	And do you do anything besides scan the photos? Like, can you make any improvements?
EMPLOYEE:	Yes, in the standard service each photo is checked, and we can sometimes <u>touch up the colour</u> a bit, or improve the contrast – that can make a big difference.
WOMAN:	OK. And some of the photos are actually quite fragile – they won't get damaged in the process, will they?
EMPLOYEE:	No, if any look particularly fragile, <u>we'd do them by hand</u>. We do realise how precious these old photos can be.
WOMAN:	Sure.
EMPLOYEE:	And another thing is we can make changes to a photo if you want – so if you want to remove an object from a photo, or maybe <u>alter the background</u>, we can do that.

Q4

Q5

Q6

Q7

WOMAN:	Really? I might be interested in that. I'll have a look through the photos and see. Oh, and talking of fixing photos – I've got a few <u>that aren't properly in focus</u>. Can you do anything to make that better?	*Q8*
EMPLOYEE:	No, I'm afraid that's one thing we can't do.	
WOMAN:	OK.	
EMPLOYEE:	Any other information I can give you?	
WOMAN:	Er … oh, how long will it all take?	
EMPLOYEE:	We aim to get the copying done <u>in ten days</u>.	*Q9*
WOMAN:	Fine. Right, well I'll get the photos packed up in a box and post them off to you.	
EMPLOYEE:	Right. If you've got a strong cardboard box, that's best. We've found that <u>plastic ones sometimes break in the post</u>.	*Q10*
WOMAN:	OK. Right, thanks for your help. Bye.	
EMPLOYEE:	Bye.	

PART 2

Good morning and thank you for coming here today. I'd like to bring you up to date with changes in the school that will affect your children.

As you know, the school buildings date from various times: some from the 1970s, some from the last five years, and of course Dartfield House is over a century old. It was commissioned by a businessman, Neville Richards, and intended as his family home, but he died before it was completed. <u>His heir chose to sell it to the local council, who turned it into offices.</u> A later plan to convert it into a tourist information centre didn't come about, through lack of money, and instead it formed the nucleus of this school when it opened 40 years ago. *Q11*

The school has grown as the local population has increased, and I can now give you some news about the lower school site, which is separated from the main site by a road. Planning permission has been granted for development of both sites. The lower school will move to new buildings that will be constructed on the main site. <u>Developers will construct houses on the existing lower school site.</u> Work on the new school buildings should start within the next few months. *Q12*

A more imminent change concerns the catering facilities and the canteen. The canteen is always very busy throughout the lunch period – in fact it's often full to capacity, because a lot of our pupils like the food that's on offer there. But there's only one serving point, so <u>most pupils have to wait a considerable time to be served</u>. This is obviously unsatisfactory, as they may have hardly finished their lunch before afternoon lessons start. *Q13*

So we've had a new Food Hall built, and this will come into use next week. It'll have several serving areas, and I'll give you more details about those in a minute, but one thing we ask you to do, to help in the smooth running of the Food Hall, is to <u>discuss with your children each morning which type of food they want to eat that day</u>, so they can go straight to the relevant serving point. There won't be any junk food – everything on offer will be healthy – and there's no change to the current system of paying for lunches by topping up your child's electronic payment card online. *Q14*

You may be wondering what will happen to the old canteen. <u>We'll still have tables and chairs in there, and pupils can eat food from the Food Hall or lunch they've brought from home.</u> Eventually we may use part of the canteen for storage, but first we'll see how many pupils go in there at lunchtime. *Q15*

OK, back to the serving points in the Food Hall, which will all have side dishes, desserts and drinks on sale, as well as main courses.

One serving point we call <u>World Adventures</u>. This will serve <u>a different country's cuisine each</u>   Q16
<u>day</u>, maybe Chinese one day and Lebanese the next. The menus will be planned for a week at a time, so pupils will know what's going to be available the whole of that week.

<u>Street Life</u> is also international, with food from three particular cultures. <u>We'll ask pupils</u>   Q17
<u>to make suggestions</u>, so perhaps sometimes there'll be food from Thailand, Ethiopia and Mexico, and then one of them will be replaced by Jamaican food for a week or two.

The <u>Speedy Italian</u> serving point <u>will cater particularly for the many pupils who don't eat meat</u>   Q18
<u>or fish</u>: they can be sure that all the food served there is suitable for them. There'll be plenty of variety, so they shouldn't get bored with the food.

OK, that's all on the new Food Hall. Now after-school lessons. These are very popular with pupils, particularly swimming – in fact there's a waiting list for lessons. Cycling is another favourite, and I'm delighted that dozens of pupils make use of the chance to learn to ride in off-road conditions. It means that more and more cycle to and from school every day. As you know, we have a well-equipped performance centre, and <u>we're going to start drama classes</u>   Q19/Q20
in there, too. Pupils will be able to join in just for fun or work up to taking part in a play – we hope to put on at least one a year. We already teach a number of pupils to use the sound and lighting systems in the centre. And a former pupil has given a magnificent grand <u>piano</u> to the school, so <u>a few pupils will be able to learn at the school instead of going to the local college</u>,   Q19/Q20
as many of them do at the moment.

PART 3

SUSIE:	So Luke, for our next psychology assignment we have to do something on sleep and dreams.
LUKE:	Right. I've just read an article suggesting why we tend to forget most of our dreams soon after we wake up. I mean, most of my dreams aren't that interesting anyway, but what it said was that if we remembered everything, <u>we might get</u> Q21 <u>mixed up about what actually happened and what we dreamed</u>. So it's a sort of protection. I hadn't heard that idea before. I'd always assumed that it was just that we didn't have room in our memories for all that stuff.
SUSIE:	Me too. What do you think about the idea that our dreams may predict the future?
LUKE:	It's a belief that you get all over the world.
SUSIE:	Yeah, lots of people have a story of it happening to them, but the explanation I've read is that <u>for each dream that comes true, we have thousands that don't</u>, Q22 but we don't notice those, we don't even remember them. We just remember the ones where something in the real world, like a view or an action, happens to trigger a dream memory.
LUKE:	Right. So <u>it's just a coincidence really</u>. Something else I read about is what they call segmented sleeping. That's a theory that hundreds of years ago, people used to get up in the middle of the night and have a chat or something to eat, then go back to bed. So I tried it myself.
SUSIE:	Why?
LUKE:	Well it's meant to make you more creative. I don't know why. But I gave it up after a week. It just didn't fit in with my lifestyle.

SUSIE:	But most pre-school children have a short sleep in the day don't they? There was an experiment some students did here last term to see at what age kids should stop having naps. But <u>they didn't really find an answer</u>. They spent a lot of time working out the most appropriate methodology, but <u>the results didn't seem to show any obvious patterns</u>.	Q23
LUKE:	Right. Anyway, let's think about our assignment. Last time <u>I had problems with the final stage, where we had to describe and justify how successful we thought we'd been</u>. I struggled a bit with the action plan too.	Q24
SUSIE:	I was OK with the planning, but <u>I got marked down for the self-assessment as well</u>. And I had big problems with the statistical stuff, that's where I really lost marks.	
LUKE:	Right.	

- -

SUSIE:	So shall we plan what we have to do for this assignment?	
LUKE:	OK.	
SUSIE:	First, we have to decide on our research question. So how about 'Is there a relationship between hours of sleep and number of dreams?'	
LUKE:	OK. Then we need to think about who we'll do the study on. About 12 people?	
SUSIE:	Right. And shall we use other psychology students?	
LUKE:	<u>Let's use people from a different department. What about history?</u>	Q25
SUSIE:	<u>Yes</u>, they might have interesting dreams! Or literature students?	
LUKE:	I don't really know any.	
SUSIE:	OK, forget that idea. Then we have to think about our methodology. So we could use observation, but that doesn't seem appropriate.	
LUKE:	No. It needs to be self-reporting I think. And we could ask them to answer questions online.	
SUSIE:	But in this case, <u>paper might be better</u> as they'll be doing it straight after they wake up … in fact while they're still half-asleep.	Q26
LUKE:	<u>Right</u>. And we'll have to <u>check the ethical guidelines</u> for this sort of research.	Q27
SUSIE:	Mm, <u>because our experiment involves humans</u>, so <u>there are special regulations</u>.	
LUKE:	Yes, I had a look at those for another assignment I did. There's a whole section on risk assessment, and another section on <u>making sure they aren't put under any unnecessary stress</u>.	Q28
SUSIE:	Let's hope they don't have any bad dreams!	
LUKE:	Yeah.	
SUSIE:	Then when we've collected all our data we have to analyse it and calculate the correlation between our two variables, that's time sleeping and number of dreams and then <u>present our results visually in a graph</u>.	Q29
LUKE:	Right. And the final thing is to think about <u>our research</u> and <u>evaluate it</u>. So that seems quite straightforward.	Q30
SUSIE:	Yeah. So now let's …	

PART 4

Dancing is something that humans do when they want to have a good time. It's a universal response to music, found in all cultures. But what's only been discovered recently is that dancing not only makes us feel good, it's also extremely good for our health.

Dancing, like other forms of exercise, releases hormones, such as dopamine, which make us feel relaxed and happy. And it also reduces feelings of stress or anxiety.

Audioscripts

Dancing is also a sociable activity, which is another reason it makes us feel good.

One study compared people's enjoyment of dancing at home in front of a video with dancing in a group in a studio.

The people dancing in a group reported feeling happier, whereas those dancing alone did not.

In another experiment, university researchers at York and Sheffield took a group of students and sent each of them into a lab where music was played for five minutes. Each had to choose from three options: to sit and listen quietly to the music, to cycle on an exercise bike while they listened, or to get up and dance. All were given cognitive tasks to perform before and after. The result showed that those who chose to dance showed much more creativity   *Q31* when doing problem-solving tasks.

Doctor Lovatt at the University of Hertfordshire believes dance could be a very useful way to help people suffering from mental health problems. He thinks dance should be prescribed as   *Q32* therapy to help people overcome issues such as depression.

It's well established that dance is a good way of encouraging adolescent girls to take exercise but what about older people? Studies have shown that there are enormous benefits for people in their sixties and beyond. One of the great things about dance is that there are no barriers to participation. Anyone can have a go, even those whose standard of fitness is   *Q33* quite low.

Dance can be especially beneficial for older adults who can't run or do more intense workouts, or for those who don't want to. One 2015 study found that even a gentle dance workout helps to promote a healthy heart. And there's plenty of evidence which suggests that dancing lowers the risk of falls, which could result in a broken hip, for example, by helping people to improve their balance.   *Q34*

There are some less obvious benefits of dance for older people too. One thing I hadn't realised before researching this topic was that dance isn't just a physical challenge. It also requires a lot of concentration because you need to remember different steps and routines. For older people, this kind of activity is especially important because it forces their brain to   *Q35* process things more quickly and to retain more information.

Current research also shows that dance promotes a general sense of well-being in older participants, which can last up to a week after a class. Participants report feeling less tired and having greater motivation to be more active and do daily activities such as gardening or   *Q36* walking to the shops or a park.

Ballroom or country dancing, both popular with older people, have to be done in groups. They require collaboration and often involve touching a dance partner, all of which encourages interaction on the dance floor. This helps to develop new relationships and can reduce older   *Q37* people's sense of isolation, which is a huge problem in many countries.

I also looked at the benefits of Zumba. Fifteen million people in 180 countries now regularly take a Zumba class, an aerobic workout based on Latin American dance moves. John Porcari, a professor of exercise and sport science at the University of Wisconsin, analysed a group of women who were Zumba regulars and found that a class lasting 40 minutes burns   *Q38* about 370 calories. This is similar to moderately intense exercises like step aerobics or kickboxing.

A study in the *American Journal of Health Behavior* showed that when <u>women with obesity</u>   *Q39*
did Zumba three times a week for 16 weeks, they <u>lost an average of 1.2 kilos and lowered</u>
<u>their percentage of body fat</u> by 1%. More importantly, the women enjoyed the class so much
that <u>they made it a habit</u> and continued to attend classes at least once a week – very unusual   *Q40*
for an aerobic exercise programme.

Dance is never going to compete with high-intensity workouts when it comes to physical
fitness gains, but its popularity is likely to keep on rising because it's such a fun way to
keep fit.

PART 1

JAKE:	Hello, Junior Cycle camp, Jake speaking.
WOMAN:	Hi. I'm calling for some information about the cycle camp – I'm thinking of sending my son.
JAKE:	Great. Well, it's held every weekday morning over the summer vacation and we focus on basic cycling skills and safety. We have eight levels for children from three years upwards. How old's your son?
WOMAN:	Charlie? He's seven. He can ride a bike, but he needs a little more training before he's safe to go on the road.
JAKE:	He'd probably be best in Level 5. They start off practising on the site here, and we aim to get them riding on the road, but first they're taken to ride in the park, away from the traffic.
WOMAN:	Right. And can you tell me a bit about the instructors?
JAKE:	Well, all our staff wear different coloured shirts. So, we have three supervisors, and they have red shirts. They support the instructors, and they also stand in for me if I'm not around. Then the instructors themselves are in blue shirts, and one of these is responsible for each class.
WOMAN:	OK.
JAKE:	In order to be accepted, all our instructors have to submit a reference from someone who's seen them work with children – like if they've worked as a babysitter, for example. Then they have to complete our training course, including how to do lesson plans, and generally care for the well-being of the kids in their class. They do a great job, I have to say.
WOMAN:	Right. And tell me a bit about the classes. What size will Charlie's class be?
JAKE:	We have a limit of eight children in each class, so their instructor really gets to know them well. They're out riding most of the time but they have quiet times too, where their instructor might tell them a story that's got something to do with cycling, or get them to play a game together. It's a lot of fun.
WOMAN:	It must be. Now, what happens if there's rain? Do the classes still run?
JAKE:	Oh yes. We don't let that put us off – we just put on our waterproofs and keep cycling.

Q1

Q2

Q3

Q4

Q5

WOMAN:	And is there anything special Charlie should bring along with him?
JAKE:	Well, maybe some spare clothes, especially if the weather's not so good. And a snack for break time.
WOMAN:	How about a drink?
JAKE:	No, we'll provide that. And make sure he has shoes, not sandals.
WOMAN:	Sure. And just at present Charlie has to take medication every few hours, so I'll make sure he has that.
JAKE:	Absolutely. Just give us details of when he has to take it and we'll make sure he does.
WOMAN:	Thanks.
JAKE:	Now, there are a few things you should know about Day 1 of the camp. The classes normally start at 9.30 every morning, but on Day 1 you should aim to get Charlie here by 9.20. The finishing time will be 12.30 as usual. We need the additional time because there are a few extra things to do. The most important is that we have a very careful check to make sure that every child's helmet fits

Q6

Q7

Q8

properly. If it doesn't fit, we'll try to adjust it, or we'll find him another one – but he must wear it all the time he's on the bike.

WOMAN: Of course.

JAKE: Then after that, all the instructors will be waiting to meet their classes, and they'll meet up in the tent – you can't miss it. And each instructor will take their class away and get started.   *Q9*

WOMAN: OK. Well that all sounds good. Now can you tell me how much the camp costs a week?

JAKE: One hundred ninety-nine dollars. We've managed to keep the price more or less the same as last year – it was one hundred ninety then. But the places are filling up quite quickly.   *Q10*

WOMAN: Right. OK, well I'd like to book for …

PART 2

Hello everyone. My name's Megan Baker and I'm a recruitment consultant at AVT Recruitment specialists.

Now, our company specialises in positions that involve working in the agriculture and horticulture sectors, so that's fresh food production, garden and park maintenance and so on. And these sectors do provide some very special career opportunities. For a start, they often offer opportunities for those who don't want to be stuck with a 40-hour week, but need to juggle work with other responsibilities such as child care – and this is very important for many of our recruits. Some people like working in a rural setting, surrounded by plants and trees instead of buildings, although we can't guarantee that. But there are certainly health benefits, especially in jobs where you're not sitting all day looking at a screen – a big plus for many people. Salaries can sometimes be good too, although there's a lot of variety here. And you may have the opportunity in some types of jobs for travel overseas, although that obviously depends on the job, and not everyone is keen to do it.   *Q11/Q12*   *Q11/Q12*

Of course, working outdoors does have its challenges. It's fine in summer, but can be extremely unpleasant when it's cold and windy. You may need to be pretty fit for some jobs, though with modern technology that's not as important as it once was. And standards of health and safety are much higher now than they used to be, so there are fewer work-related accidents. But if you like a lively city environment surrounded by lots of people, these jobs are probably not for you – they're often in pretty remote areas. And some people worry about finding a suitable place to live, but in our experience, this usually turns out fine.   *Q13/Q14*   *Q13/Q14*

Now let me tell you about some of the exciting jobs that we have on our books right now.

One is for a fresh food commercial manager. Our client here is a very large fresh food producer supplying a range of top supermarkets. They operate in a very fast-paced environment with low profit margins – the staff there work hard, but they play hard as well, so if you've a sociable personality this may be for you.   *Q15*

We have an exciting post as an agronomist advising farmers on issues such as crop nutrition, protection against pests, and the latest legislation on farming and agricultural practices. There are good opportunities for the right person to quickly make their way up the career ladder, but a deep knowledge of the agricultural sector is expected of applicants.   *Q16*

A leading supermarket is looking for a fresh produce buyer who is available for a 12-month maternity cover contract. You need to have experience in administration, planning and buying in the fresh produce industry, and in return will receive a very competitive salary.   *Q17*

We have also received a request for a <u>sales manager for a chain of garden centres</u>. You will <u>be visiting centres in the region</u> to ensure their high levels of customer service are maintained. This post is only suitable for someone who is prepared to live in the region.

Q18

There is also a vacancy for a <u>tree technician</u> to carry out tree cutting, forestry and conservation work. Candidates must have a clean driving licence and have training in safety procedures. A year's experience would be preferred but <u>the company might be prepared to consider someone who has just completed an appropriate training course</u>.

Q19

Finally, we have a position for a <u>farm worker</u>. This will involve a wide range of farm duties including crop sowing and harvesting, machine maintenance and animal care. Perks of the job include <u>the possibility of renting a small cottage on the estate</u>, and the chance to earn a competitive salary. A driving licence and tractor driving experience are essential.

Q20

PART 3

ADAM:	OK Rosie, shall we try to get some ideas together for our presentation on diet and obesity?
ROSIE:	Sure.
ADAM:	I can talk about the experiment I did to see if people can tell the difference between real sugar and artificial sweeteners.
ROSIE:	Where you gave people drinks with either sugar or artificial sweeteners and they had to say which they thought it was?
ADAM:	Yeah. It took me ages to decide exactly how I'd organise it, especially how I could make sure that <u>people didn't know which drink I was giving them</u>. It was hard to keep track of it all, especially as <u>I had so many people doing it</u> – I had to make sure I kept a proper record of what each person had had.
ROSIE:	So could most people tell the difference?
ADAM:	Yeah – I hadn't thought they would be able to, but most people could.
ROSIE:	Then there's that experiment I did measuring the fat content of nuts, to see if the nutritional information given on the packet was accurate.
ADAM:	The one where you ground up the nuts and mixed them with a chemical to absorb the fat?
ROSIE:	Yes. My results were a bit problematic – the fat content for that type of nut seemed much lower than it said on the package. But I reckon the package information was right. I think <u>I should probably have ground up the nuts more than I did</u>. <u>It's possible that the scales for weighing the fat weren't accurate enough</u>, too. I'd really like to try the experiment again some time.

Q21/Q22
Q21/Q22

Q23/Q24
Q23/Q24

ADAM:	So what can we say about helping people to lose weight? There's a lot we could say about what restaurants could do to reduce obesity. I read that the items at the start of a menu and the items at the end of a menu are much more likely to be chosen than the items in the middle. So, <u>if you put the low-calorie items at the beginning and end of the menu, people will probably go for the food with fewer calories</u>, without even realising what they're doing.
ROSIE:	I think food *manufacturers* could do more to encourage healthy eating.
ADAM:	How?
ROSIE:	Well, <u>when manufacturers put calorie counts of a food on the label, they're sometimes really confusing and I suspect they do it on purpose</u>. Because food that's high in calories tastes better, and so they'll sell more.

Q25

Q26

ADAM:	Yeah, so if you look at the amount of calories in a pizza, they'll give you the calories per quarter pizza and you think, oh that's not too bad. But who's going to eat a quarter pizza?	
ROSIE:	Exactly.	
ADAM:	I suppose another approach to this problem is to get people to exercise more.	
ROSIE:	Right. In England, the current guidelines are for at least 30 minutes of brisk walking, five days a week. Now when you ask them, <u>about 40% of men and 30% of women say they do this, but when you objectively measure the amount of walking they do with motion sensors, you find that only 6% of men and 4% of women do the recommended amount of exercise.</u>	*Q27*
ADAM:	Mm, so you can see why obesity is growing.	
ROSIE:	So how can people be encouraged to take more exercise?	
ADAM:	Well, for example, think of the location of stairs in a train station. <u>If people reach the stairs before they reach the escalator when they're leaving the station, they're more likely to take the stairs. And if you increase the *width* of the stairs, you'll get more people using them at the same time.</u> It's an unconscious process and influenced by minor modifications in their environment.	*Q28*
ROSIE:	Right. And it might not be a big change, but if it happens every day, it all adds up.	
ADAM:	Yes. But actually, <u>I'm not sure if we should be talking about exercise in our presentation.</u>	*Q29*
ROSIE:	Well, we've done quite a bit of reading about it.	
ADAM:	I know, but it's going to mean we have a very wide focus, and our tutor did say that <u>we need to focus on causes and solutions in terms of nutrition.</u>	
ROSIE:	<u>I suppose so. And we've got plenty of information about that.</u> OK, well that will be simpler.	
ADAM:	So what shall we do now? We've still got half an hour before our next lecture.	
ROSIE:	<u>Let's think about what we're going to include and what will go where.</u> Then we can decide what slides we need.	*Q30*
ADAM:	OK, fine.	

PART 4

Good morning everyone. So today we're going to look at an important creative activity and that's hand knitting. Ancient knitted garments have been found in many different countries, showing that knitting is a global activity with a long history.

When someone says the word 'knitting' <u>we might well picture an elderly person – a grandmother perhaps – sitting by the fire knitting</u> garments for themselves or other members of the family. It's a homely image, but one that may lead you to feel that knitting is an activity of the past – and, indeed, <u>during the previous decade, it was one of the skills that was predicted to vanish</u> from everyday life. For although humans have sewn and knitted their own clothing for a very long time, many of these craft-based skills went into decline when industrial machines took over – mainly because they were no longer passed down from one generation to another. However, that's all changing and interest in knitting classes in many countries is actually rising, as more and more people are seeking formal instruction in the skill. With that trend, we're also seeing <u>an increase in the sales figures for knitting equipment</u>.   *Q33*

So why do people want to be taught to knit at a time when a machine can readily do the job for them? The answer is that knitting, as a handicraft, has numerous benefits for those doing it. Let's consider what some of these might be. While many people knitted garments in the past because they couldn't afford to buy clothes, it's still true today that <u>knitting can be helpful if you're experiencing economic hardship</u>. If you have several children who all need warm

Q31

Q32

Q34

winter clothes, knitting may save you a lot of money. And the results of knitting your own clothes can be very rewarding, even though <u>the skills you need to get going are really quite basic</u> and the financial outlay is minimal.

Q35

But the more significant benefits in today's world are to do with well-being. In a world where it's estimated that we spend up to nine hours a day online, doing something with our hands that is craft-based makes us feel good. It releases us from the stress of a technological, fast-paced life.

Now, let's look back a bit to early knitting activities. In fact, no one really knows when knitting first began, but archaeological remains have disclosed plenty of information for us to think about.

One of the interesting things about knitting is that the earliest pieces of clothing that have been found suggest that <u>most of the items produced were round</u> rather than flat. Discoveries from the 3rd and 4th centuries in Egypt show that things like socks and gloves, that were needed to keep hands and feet warm, were knitted in one piece using four or five needles. That's very different from most knitting patterns today, which only require two. What's more, the very first needles people used were hand carved out of wood and <u>other natural materials, like bone</u>, whereas today's needles are largely made of steel or plastic and make that characteristic clicking sound when someone's using them. Ancient people knitted using yarns made from linen, hemp, cotton and wool, and <u>these were often very rough on the skin</u>. The spinning wheel, which allowed people to make finer yarns and produce much greater quantities of them, led to the dominance of wool in the knitting industry – often favoured for its warmth.

Q36

Q37

Q38

Another interesting fact about knitting is that because it was practised in so many parts of the world for so many purposes, <u>regional differences in style developed</u>. This visual identity has allowed researchers to match bits of knitted clothing that have been unearthed over time to the region from which the wearer came or the job that he or she did.

Q39

As I've mentioned, knitting offered people from poor communities a way of making extra money while doing other tasks. For many centuries, it seems, men, women and children took every opportunity to knit, for example, while <u>watching over sheep</u>, walking to market or riding in boats. So, let's move on to take a …

Q40

TEST 4

PART 1

SHIRLEY:	Hello?
TOM:	Oh hello. I was hoping to speak to Jack Fitzgerald about renting a cottage.
SHIRLEY:	I'm his wife, Shirley, and we own the cottages together, so I'm sure I can help you.
TOM:	Great. My name's Tom. Some friends of ours rented Granary Cottage from you last year, and they thought it was great. So my wife and I are hoping to come in May for a week.
SHIRLEY:	What date did you have in mind?
TOM:	The week beginning the 14th, if possible.
SHIRLEY:	I'll just check … I'm sorry, Tom, it's already booked that week. It's free the week beginning the 28th, though, for seven nights. In fact, that's the only time you could have it in May.

Q1 appears beside the line about the week beginning the 28th.

TOM:	Oh. Well, we could manage that, I think. We'd just need to change a couple of things. How much would it cost?
SHIRLEY:	That's the beginning of high season, so it'd be £550 for the week.

Q2 appears beside the £550 line.

TOM:	Ah. That's a bit more than we wanted to pay, I'm afraid. We've budgeted up to £500 for accommodation.
SHIRLEY:	Well, we've just finished converting another building into a cottage, which we're calling Chervil Cottage.

Q3 appears beside the Chervil Cottage line.

TOM:	Sorry? What was that again?
SHIRLEY:	Chervil. C-H-E-R-V for Victor I-L.
TOM:	Oh, that's a herb, isn't it?
SHIRLEY:	That's right. It grows fairly wild around here. You could have that for the week you want for £480.
TOM:	OK. So could you tell me something about it, please?
SHIRLEY:	Of course. The building was built as a garage. It's a little smaller than Granary Cottage.

Q4 appears beside the "built as a garage" line.

TOM:	So that must sleep two people, as well?
SHIRLEY:	That's right. There's a double bedroom.
TOM:	Does it have a garden?

Q5 appears beside the "garden" line.

SHIRLEY:	Yes, you get to it from the living room through French doors, and we provide two deckchairs. We hope to build a patio in the near future, but I wouldn't like to guarantee it'll be finished by May.
TOM:	OK.
SHIRLEY:	The front door opens onto the old farmyard, and parking isn't a problem – there's plenty of room at the front for that. There are some trees and potted plants there.

Q6 appears beside the parking line.

TOM:	What about facilities in the cottage? It has standard things like a cooker and fridge, I presume.
SHIRLEY:	In the kitchen area there's a fridge-freezer and we've just put in an electric cooker.
TOM:	Is there a washing machine?
SHIRLEY:	Yes. There's also a TV in the living room, which plays DVDs too. The bathroom is too small for a bath, so there's a shower instead. I think a lot of people prefer that nowadays, anyway.

TOM:	It's more environmentally friendly, isn't it? Unless you spend half the day in it!
SHIRLEY:	Exactly.
TOM:	What about heating? It sometimes gets quite cool at that time of year.
SHIRLEY:	There's central heating, and if you want to light a fire, <u>there's a stove. We can provide all the wood you need for it.</u> It smells so much nicer than coal, and it makes the room very cosy – we've got one in our own house.

Q7

TOM:	That sounds very pleasant. Perhaps we should come in the winter, to make the most of it!
SHIRLEY:	Yes, we find we don't want to go out when we've got the fire burning. There are some attractive views from the cottage, which I haven't mentioned. There's <u>a famous stone bridge – it's one of the oldest</u> in the region, and <u>you can see it from the living room</u>. It isn't far away. <u>The bedroom window looks in the opposite direction, and has a lovely view of the hills and the monument at the top.</u>

Q8
Q9

TOM:	Well, that all sounds perfect. I'd like to book it, please. Would you want a deposit?
SHIRLEY:	Yes, we ask for thirty percent to secure your booking, so that'll be, um, £144.
TOM:	And when would you like the rest of the money?
SHIRLEY:	You're coming in May, so <u>the last day of March, please.</u>

Q10

TOM:	Fine.
SHIRLEY:	Excellent. Could I just take your details ...

PART 2

CHAIRPERSON:	Right. Next on the agenda we have traffic and highways. Councillor Thornton.
COUNCILLOR THORNTON:	Thank you. Well, we now have the results of the survey carried out last month about traffic and road transport in the town. People were generally satisfied with the state of the roads. There were one or two complaints about potholes which will be addressed, but <u>a significant number of people complained about the increasing number of heavy vehicles</u> using our local roads to avoid traffic elsewhere. We'd expected more complaints by commuters about the reduction in the train service, but it doesn't seem to have affected people too much. The cycle path that runs alongside the river is very well used by both cyclists and pedestrians since the surface was improved last year, but overtaking can be a problem so <u>we're going to add a bit on the side to make it wider</u>. At some stage, we'd like to extend the path so that it goes all the way through the town, but that won't be happening in the immediate future.

Q11

Q12

	The plans to have a pedestrian crossing next to the Post Office have unfortunately had to be put on hold for the time being. We'd budgeted for this to be done this financial year, but then there were rumours that the Post Office was going to move, which would have meant there wasn't really a need for a crossing. Now they've confirmed that they're staying where they are, but the Highways Department have told us that <u>it would be dangerous to have a pedestrian crossing where we'd originally planned it as there's a bend in the road there</u>. So that'll need some more thought. On Station Road near the station and level crossing, drivers can face quite <u>long waits if the level crossing's closed</u>, and <u>we've now got signs up requesting them not to leave their engines running at that time</u>. This means pedestrians waiting on the pavement to cross

Q13

Q14

the railway line don't have to breathe in car fumes. We've had some problems with cyclists leaving their bikes chained to the railings outside the ticket office, but the station has agreed to provide bike racks there.

CHAIRPERSON:	So next on the agenda is 'Proposals for improvements to the recreation ground'. Councillor Thornton again.
COUNCILLOR THORNTON:	Well, since we managed to extend the recreation ground, we've spent some time talking to local people about how it could be made a more attractive and useful space. If you have a look at the map up on the screen, you can see the river up in the north, and the Community Hall near the entrance from the road. At present, cars can park between the Community Hall and that line of trees to the east, but this is quite dangerous for pedestrians so we're suggesting a new car park on the opposite side of the Community Hall, right next to it.

Q15

We also have a new location for the cricket pitch. As we've now purchased additional space to the east of the recreation ground, beyond the trees, we plan to move it away from its current location, which is rather near the road, into this new area beyond the line of trees. This means there's less danger of stray balls hitting cars or pedestrians.

Q16

We've got plans for a children's playground which will be accessible by a footpath from the Community Hall and will be alongside the river. We'd originally thought of having it close to the road, but we think this will be a more attractive location.

Q17

The skateboard ramp is very popular with both younger and older children – we had considered moving this up towards the river, but in the end we decided to have it in the southeast corner near the road.

Q18

The pavilion is very well used at present by both football players and cricketers. It will stay where it is now – to the left of the line of trees and near to the river – handy for both the football and cricket pitches.

Q19

And finally, we'll be getting a new notice board for local information, and that will be directly on people's right as they go from the road into the recreation ground.

Q20

PART 3

JAKE:	Now that we've done all the research into bike-sharing schemes in cities around the world, we need to think about how we're going to organise our report.
AMY:	Right. I think we should start by talking about the benefits. I mean it's great that so many cities have introduced these schemes where anyone can pick up a bike from dozens of different locations and hire it for a few hours. It makes riding a bike very convenient for people.
JAKE:	Yes, but the costs can add up and that puts people on low incomes off in some places.
AMY:	I suppose so, but if it means more people in general are cycling rather than driving, then because they're increasing the amount of physical activity they do, it's good for their health.
JAKE:	OK. But isn't that of less importance? I mean, doesn't the impact of reduced emissions on air pollution have a more significant effect on people's health?

Q21/Q22

AMY:	Certainly, in some cities bike-sharing has made a big contribution to that. And also helped to cut the number of cars on the road significantly.	Q21/Q22
JAKE:	Which is the main point.	
AMY:	Exactly. But I'd say it's had less of an impact on noise pollution because there are still loads of buses and lorries around.	
JAKE:	Right.	
AMY:	Shall we quickly discuss the recommendations we're going to make?	
JAKE:	In order to ensure bike-sharing schemes are successful?	
AMY:	Yes.	
JAKE:	OK. Well, while I think it's nice to have really state-of-the art bikes with things like GPS, I wouldn't say they're absolutely necessary.	
AMY:	But some technical things are really important – like a fully functional app – so people can make payments and book bikes easily. Places which haven't invested in that have really struggled.	Q23/Q24
JAKE:	Good point … Some people say there shouldn't be competing companies offering separate bike-sharing schemes, but in some really big cities, competition's beneficial and anyway one company might not be able to manage the whole thing.	
AMY:	Right. Deciding how much to invest is a big question. Cities which have opened loads of new bike lanes at the same time as introducing bike-sharing schemes have generally been more successful – but there are examples of successful schemes where this hasn't happened … What does matter though – is having a big publicity campaign.	Q23/Q24
JAKE:	Definitely. If people don't know how to use the scheme or don't understand its benefits, they won't use it. People need a lot of persuasion to stop using their cars.	

AMY:	Shall we look at some examples now? And say what we think is good or bad about them.	
JAKE:	I suppose we should start with Amsterdam as this was one of the first cities to have a bike-sharing scheme.	
AMY:	Yes. There was already a strong culture of cycling here. In a way it's strange that there was such a demand for bike-sharing because you'd have thought most people would have used their own bikes.	Q25
JAKE:	And yet it's one of the best-used schemes … Dublin's an interesting example of a success story.	
AMY:	It must be because the public transport system's quite limited.	Q26
JAKE:	Not really – there's no underground, but there are trams and a good bus network. I'd say price has a lot to do with it. It's one of the cheapest schemes in Europe to join.	
AMY:	But the buses are really slow – anyway the weather certainly can't be a factor!	
JAKE:	No – definitely not. The London scheme's been quite successful.	
AMY:	Yes – it's been a really good thing for the city. The bikes are popular and the whole system is well maintained but it isn't expanding quickly enough.	
JAKE:	Basically, not enough's been spent on increasing the number of cycle lanes. Hopefully that'll change.	Q27
AMY:	Yes. Now what about outside Europe?	
JAKE:	Well bike-sharing schemes have taken off in places like Buenos Aires.	
AMY:	Mmm. They built a huge network of cycle lanes to support the introduction of the scheme there, didn't they? It attracted huge numbers of cyclists where previously there were hardly any.	
JAKE:	An example of good planning.	Q28

AMY:	Absolutely. New York is a good example of how not to introduce a scheme. When they launched it, <u>it was more than ten times the price of most other schemes</u>.	
JAKE:	<u>More than it costs to take a taxi. Crazy.</u> I think the organisers lacked vision and ambition there.	*Q29*
AMY:	I think so too. Sydney would be a good example to use. <u>I would have expected it to have grown pretty quickly here.</u>	*Q30*
JAKE:	Yes. <u>I can't quite work out why it hasn't been an instant success</u> like some of the others. It's a shame really.	
AMY:	I know. OK so now we've thought about …	

PART 4

One of the most famous cases of extinction is that of a bird known as the dodo. In fact there's even a saying in English, 'as dead as the dodo', used to refer to something which no longer exists. But for many centuries the dodo was alive and well, although it could only be found in one place, the island of Mauritius in the Indian Ocean. It was a very large bird, about one metre tall, and over the centuries it had lost the ability to fly, but it survived happily under the trees that covered the island.

Then in the year 1507 the first Portuguese ships stopped at the island. The sailors were carrying <u>spices</u> back to Europe, and found the island a convenient stopping place where *Q31* they could stock up with food and water for the rest of the voyage, but they didn't settle on Mauritius. However, in 1638 the Dutch arrived and set up a <u>colony</u> there. These first human *Q32* inhabitants of the island found the dodo birds a convenient source of meat, although not everyone liked the taste.

It's hard to get an accurate description of what the dodo actually looked like. We do have some written records from sailors, and a few pictures, but we don't know how reliable these are. The best-known picture is a Dutch painting in which the bird appears to be extremely <u>fat</u>, but this may not be accurate – an Indian painting done at the same time shows a much *Q33* thinner bird.

Although attempts were made to preserve the bodies of some of the birds, no complete specimen survives. In the early 17th century four dried parts of a bird were known to exist – of these, three have disappeared, so only one example of soft tissue from the dodo survives, a dodo <u>head</u>. Bones have also been found, but there's only one complete skeleton in existence. *Q34*

This single dodo skeleton has recently been the subject of scientific research which suggests that many of the earlier beliefs about dodos may have been incorrect. For example, early accounts of the birds mention how slow and clumsy it was, but scientists now believe the bird's strong knee joints would have made it capable of <u>movement</u> which was not slow, but *Q35* actually quite fast. In fact, one 17th century sailor wrote that he found the birds hard to catch. It's true that the dodo's small wings wouldn't have allowed it to leave the ground, but the scientists suggest that these were probably employed for <u>balance</u> while going over uneven *Q36* ground. Another group of scientists carried out analysis of the dodo's skull. They found that the reports of the lack of intelligence of the dodo were not borne out by their research, which suggested the bird's <u>brain</u> was not small, but average in size. In fact, in relation to its *Q37* body size, it was similar to that of the pigeon, which is known to be a highly intelligent bird. The researchers also found that the structure of the bird's skull suggested that one sense which was particularly well-developed was that of <u>smell</u>. So the dodo may also have been *Q38* particularly good at locating ripe fruit and other food in the island's thick vegetation.

So it looks as if the dodo was better able to survive and defend itself than was originally believed. Yet less than 200 years after Europeans first arrived on the island, they had become extinct. So what was the reason for this? For a long time, it was believed that the dodos were hunted to extinction, but scientists now believe the situation was more complicated than this. Another factor may have been the new species brought to the island by the sailors. These included dogs, which would have been a threat to the dodos, and also monkeys, which ate the fruit that was the main part of the dodos' diet. These were brought to the island deliberately, but the ships also brought another type of creature – <u>rats</u>, which *Q39* came to land from the ships and rapidly overran the island. These upset the ecology of the island, not just the dodos but other species too. However, they were a particular danger to the dodos because they consumed their eggs, and since each dodo only laid one at a time, this probably had a devastating effect on populations.

However, we now think that probably the main cause of the birds' extinction was not the introduction of non-native species, but the introduction of agriculture. This meant that the <u>forest</u> that had once covered all the island, and that had provided a perfect home for the *Q40* dodo, was cut down so that crops such as sugar could be grown. So although the dodo had survived for thousands of years, suddenly it was gone.

Listening and Reading answer keys

TEST 1

LISTENING

 Answer key with extra explanations in Resource Bank

30
7.0

Part 1, Questions 1–10

1 egg
2 tower
3 car
4 animals
5 bridge
6 movie / film
7 decorate
8 Wednesdays
9 Fradstone
10 parking

Part 2, Questions 11–20

11 C
12 A
13 B
14 C
15 H
16 C
17 G
18 B
19 I
20 A

Part 3, Questions 21–30

21&22 *IN EITHER ORDER*
    C
    E
23&24 *IN EITHER ORDER*
    B
    E
25 D
26 C
27 A
28 H
29 F
30 G

Part 4, Questions 31–40

31 practical
32 publication
33 choices
34 negative
35 play
36 capitalism
37 depression
38 logic
39 opportunity
40 practice / practise

If you score …

1–17	18–27	28–40
you are unlikely to get an acceptable score under examination conditions and we recommend that you spend a lot of time improving your English before you take IELTS.	you may get an acceptable score under examination conditions but we recommend that you think about having more practice or lessons before you take IELTS.	you are likely to get an acceptable score under examination conditions but remember that different institutions will find different scores acceptable.

TEST 1

READING

 Answer key with extra explanations
in Resource Bank

Reading Section 1,
Questions 1–14

1 D
2 B
3 C
4 E
5 A
6 B
7 TRUE
8 TRUE
9 NOT GIVEN
10 FALSE
11 FALSE
12 FALSE
13 TRUE
14 NOT GIVEN

Reading Section 2,
Questions 15–27

15 fertiliser / fertilizer
16 animal
17 obstacle
18 aids
19 bending
20 gate

21 proactive
22 special offers
23 brand names
24 negativity
25 presentation
26 credit card
27 rudeness

Reading Section 3,
Questions 28–40

28 vi
29 iv
30 ii
31 viii
32 v
33 i
34 iii
35 D
36 D
37 A
38 family
39 platform
40 multi(-)coloured / multi(-)colored

If you score ...

1–25	26–33	34–40
you are unlikely to get an acceptable score under examination conditions and we recommend that you spend a lot of time improving your English before you take IELTS.	you may get an acceptable score under examination conditions but we recommend that you think about having more practice or lessons before you take IELTS.	you are likely to get an acceptable score under examination conditions but remember that different institutions will find different scores acceptable.

TEST 2

LISTENING

 Answer key with extra explanations in Resource Bank

Part 1, Questions 1–10

1   frame
2   195
3   payment
4   Grandparents
5   colour / color
6   hand
7   background
8   focus
9   ten / 10 days
10 plastic

Part 2, Questions 11–20

11 C
12 B
13 A
14 A
15 C
16 D
17 A
18 B
19&20 *IN EITHER ORDER*
    B
    C

Part 3, Questions 21–30

21 B
22 A
23 C
24 C
25 history
26 paper
27 humans / people
28 stress
29 graph
30 evaluate

Part 4, Questions 31–40

31 creativity
32 therapy
33 fitness
34 balance
35 brain
36 motivation
37 isolation
38 calories
39 obesity
40 habit

If you score ...

1–18	19–28	29–40
you are unlikely to get an acceptable score under examination conditions and we recommend that you spend a lot of time improving your English before you take IELTS.	you may get an acceptable score under examination conditions but we recommend that you think about having more practice or lessons before you take IELTS.	you are likely to get an acceptable score under examination conditions but remember that different institutions will find different scores acceptable.

TEST 2

READING

 Answer key with extra explanations in Resource Bank

Reading Section 1, Questions 1–14

1   FALSE
2   TRUE
3   NOT GIVEN
4   TRUE
5   FALSE
6   TRUE
7   FALSE
8   F
9   H
10 C
11 F
12 A
13 D
14 E

Reading Section 2, Questions 15–27

15 festivals
16 budget
17 partnerships
18 diversity
19 database
20 accounting

21 knowledge
22 regulations
23 responsibilities
24 leaflets
25 statement
26 contractors
27 stress

Reading Section 3, Questions 28–40

28 B
29 A
30 C
31 B
32 D
33 C
34 F
35 B
36 A
37 community service
38 shifting sand
39 copper
40 farmers

If you score ...

1–25	26–32	33–40
you are unlikely to get an acceptable score under examination conditions and we recommend that you spend a lot of time improving your English before you take IELTS.	you may get an acceptable score under examination conditions but we recommend that you think about having more practice or lessons before you take IELTS.	you are likely to get an acceptable score under examination conditions but remember that different institutions will find different scores acceptable.

TEST 3

LISTENING

 Answer key with extra explanations in Resource Bank

Part 1, Questions 1–10

1 park
2 blue
3 reference
4 story
5 rain
6 snack
7 medication
8 helmet
9 tent
10 199

Part 2, Questions 11–20

11&12 *IN EITHER ORDER*
  A
  C
13&14 *IN EITHER ORDER*
  B
  C
15 D
16 F
17 A
18 H
19 C
20 G

Part 3, Questions 21–30

21&22 *IN EITHER ORDER*
  C
  D
23&24 *IN EITHER ORDER*
  C
  E
25 C
26 A
27 B
28 A
29 A
30 C

Part 4, Questions 31–40

31 grandmother
32 decade
33 equipment
34 economic
35 basic
36 round
37 bone
38 rough
39 style
40 sheep

If you score ...

1–18	19–27	28–40
you are unlikely to get an acceptable score under examination conditions and we recommend that you spend a lot of time improving your English before you take IELTS.	you may get an acceptable score under examination conditions but we recommend that you think about having more practice or lessons before you take IELTS.	you are likely to get an acceptable score under examination conditions but remember that different institutions will find different scores acceptable.

TEST 3

READING

 Answer key with extra explanations in Resource Bank

Reading Section 1, Questions 1–14

1	E
2	D
3	C
4	A
5	C
6	TRUE
7	NOT GIVEN
8	NOT GIVEN
9	FALSE
10	TRUE
11	TRUE
12	NOT GIVEN
13	FALSE
14	FALSE

Reading Section 2, Questions 15–27

15	correct
16	conversation
17	filter
18	fresh
19	flavour / flavor
20	bitter
21	day
22	issues
23	(relevant) information
24	(meeting) agenda
25	conflicts
26	tension
27	social activity

Reading Section 3, Questions 28–40

28	vii
29	iii
30	i
31	vi
32	viii
33	v
34	B
35	C
36	B
37	C
38	G
39	E
40	B

If you score …

1–25	26–32	33–40
you are unlikely to get an acceptable score under examination conditions and we recommend that you spend a lot of time improving your English before you take IELTS.	you may get an acceptable score under examination conditions but we recommend that you think about having more practice or lessons before you take IELTS.	you are likely to get an acceptable score under examination conditions but remember that different institutions will find different scores acceptable.

TEST 4

LISTENING

 Answer key with extra explanations in Resource Bank

Part 1, Questions 1–10

1 28th
2 550
3 Chervil
4 garage
5 garden
6 parking
7 wood
8 bridge
9 monument
10 March

Part 2, Questions 11–20

11 C
12 A
13 B
14 B
15 C
16 F
17 A
18 I
19 E
20 H

Part 3, Questions 21–30

21&22 *IN EITHER ORDER*
    B
    C
23&24 *IN EITHER ORDER*
    B
    C
25 C
26 F
27 D
28 E
29 B
30 A

Part 4, Questions 31–40

31 spice(s)
32 colony / settlement
33 fat
34 head
35 movement
36 balance / balancing
37 brain
38 smell
39 rats
40 forest

If you score …

1–18	19–27	28–40
you are unlikely to get an acceptable score under examination conditions and we recommend that you spend a lot of time improving your English before you take IELTS.	you may get an acceptable score under examination conditions but we recommend that you think about having more practice or lessons before you take IELTS.	you are likely to get an acceptable score under examination conditions but remember that different institutions will find different scores acceptable.

TEST 4

READING

 Answer key with extra explanations in Resource Bank

Reading Section 1, Questions 1–14

1	D
2	B
3	A
4	C
5	F
6	C
7	E
8	G
9	FALSE
10	NOT GIVEN
11	NOT GIVEN
12	FALSE
13	TRUE
14	FALSE

Reading Section 2, Questions 15–27

15	highlight
16	details
17	insights
18	samples
19	questionnaire
20	authentic
21	routine
22	dress code
23	personalities
24	conversation starters
25	goals
26	open mind
27	improvements

Reading Section 3, Questions 28–40

28	D
29	C
30	A
31	D
32	C
33	B
34	A
35	D
36	C
37	A
38	grounds
39	referees
40	prejudice

If you score ...

1–25	26–32	33–40
you are unlikely to get an acceptable score under examination conditions and we recommend that you spend a lot of time improving your English before you take IELTS.	you may get an acceptable score under examination conditions but we recommend that you think about having more practice or lessons before you take IELTS.	you are likely to get an acceptable score under examination conditions but remember that different institutions will find different scores acceptable.

Sample Writing answers

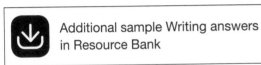

TEST 1, WRITING TASK 1

This is an answer written by a candidate who achieved a **Band 5.5** score.

Good morning Mrs Barrett. My name is Alfonso Jose Suaza I'm from Colombia. I saw your advertised that you are looking for someone to help you in your home for a few hours a day next summer. Also I'm really interested to get this opportunity. A few years ago I was working as a cook in a Hotel, so I can help you in domestic task in your house and made your meals for breakfast, lunch and dinner. Forthemore I enjoyed to work in the hospitality and the cookery is my passion I love making food for everyone this make me happy. Actually I'm am international student, so I go to the school in southport at the afternoon Monday to Friday from 1:30 till 5:30, and free on the weekend, I'm able in the mornings and weekends. Thanks for your time

Kind regrets,

Dear Mrs Barrett

Here is the examiner's comment:

> The writer has addressed each of the bullet points, although more details could have been given, as they only mention cooking and no other ways to help. However, there is a clear progression which follows the order of the bullet points in the question. We can see the format is appropriate for a letter but there are errors at the close [*Kind regrets* | *Dear Mrs Barrett*].

> Vocabulary is generally adequate for the task [*opportunity* | *cookery is my passion* | *make me happy*] although some is taken from the question and there are errors in word choice [*able* / available | *regrets* / regards]. There are some attempts at complex structures (using relative pronouns) but the range is limited. The Band Score could be improved if spelling and word choice were more accurate and if there was more variety of sentence structures.

TEST 1, WRITING TASK 2

This is an answer written by a candidate who achieved a **Band 7.0** score.

Nowadays, our environment suffers from plastic packaging and plastic bags, plastic does a great damage to the planet. In this essay, the actions how to solve the plastic problem will be mentioned and what can be done to lower the use of plastic packaging will be discussed.

Firstly, plastic products are usually thrown under the ground, so that it is able to cause ground pollution, the soil becomes poor. It is one of the reasons why trees and plants do not grow as they used to fifty years ago. Secondly, production of plastic causes air pollution. Factories that produce plastic bags, packaging and other plastic products emmit exhaust fumes to the atmosphere. All of the facts mentioned can prove that plastic pollution plays the leading role in the list of environmental problems.

What pollution abutement can be done to lower the risk of Earth damaging? First, plastic bags can be changed to bags made of natural materials like clothes of wood. To realize this, factories should lower the production of plastic bags and change them to more natural products. Moreover, the problem of ground pollution because of plastic production should be discussed in social media to let people know the scope of plastic problem. Second, already used plastic can be recycled in other products. There is a Russian programm of recycling plastic into T-shirts, caps and even balls for football and basketball.

In conclusion, I would like to say that, nowadays, people appear as the main reason of environmental problems, the manufacturing of plastic products increases the risk of the further Earth life. Everything should be done to lower the risk of destroying the planet.

Here is the examiner's comment:

This is a strong response which addresses all parts of the task. It has an introduction to the topic, refers to ground and air pollution and presents solutions to address the problems identified. To score more highly, there could be a clearer outline of what 'governments' and 'individuals' can do. Ideas are logically organised into four paragraphs, including an introduction and a conclusion. Within the paragraphs, we can see sequencing [*Firstly | Secondly*] and other cohesive devices [*Moreover | In conclusion*], as well as some effective referencing [*All of the facts mentioned | change them*].

There is a wide range of vocabulary and evidence of the ability to convey precise meanings [*exhaust fumes | leading role | scope | risk of destroying the planet*]. There are occasional errors in spelling [*emmit* / emit | *abutement* / abatement | *programm* / programme] but generally good control over word choice.

The writing also shows a variety of complex grammatical structures with frequent error-free sentences. We can see a range of tenses, including modal forms [*can prove that | should be done*]. There are a few errors remaining, e.g., with articles [*plastic does a great damage | scope of plastic problem*] and prepositions [*main reason of* / main reason for].

TEST 2, WRITING TASK 1

This is an answer written by a candidate who achieved a **Band 6.5** score.

Dear Sir or Madam,

I am writing you because I would like to give you my opinion on your article about town centres which you published in a national newspaper called Denik.

First of all I have to agree with the part where you mentioned a shape and an organization of main squares. Most of them have a rounded shape with lots of different shops around and to a fountain in the center.

However, I found the center of Brno quite different from most of other cities. Mostly because it has nice older architecture combined with modern style. Brno has also one unique difference that is that a tram goes right across of the middle of the main square. Also the main train station together with tram station is placed right under the main square, which is not so common in other cities.

At the end, I would like to offer a tour in Brno in hope that it could change your opinion. If you decide to visit my town, please don't hesitate to contact me. I will be more than happy to show you the beauty of this city.

Yours faithfully,

Here is the examiner's comment:

> All three bullet points are addressed and the tone is polite in this letter to a newspaper. In this task, the bullet points ask 'which points / explain ways' (plural) which means more than one point or example is required per bullet point. In this response, two examples are provided for each of the first two bullet points, satisfying the requirements for this task.*

> Progression is clear and cohesive devices are used well [*which you published | Most of them | that is that*]. There are some inaccuracies [*At the end / finally*]. The range of vocabulary does allow some flexibility [*mentioned | architecture combined with modern style | unique difference | not so common | change your opinion*]. However, a wider range would be needed to score more highly here. Similarly, complex sentence forms are attempted, but generally sentences are short and flexibility is limited in this response.

Note

*It is important for test takers to notice if more than one example is required for each bullet point (e.g., problem<u>s</u>, point<u>s</u>, way<u>s</u>, example<u>s</u>) because if only one is provided, this is not a complete response to the question.

TEST 2, WRITING TASK 2

This is an answer written by a candidate who achieved a **Band 5.5** score.

Some people prefer to keep to things that they can or use to. I think it has good side and bad side.

First of all, keep to do same thing make you forcus to things. You can learn and enjoy deeply. Also, keep to do same thing makes you comfortable. You can relax to do it. If you have bad day, you don't need to look for what makes you relax because you already used to do it. For example, you can watch film, visit place, eat food whatever you like or used to. You can go back your routines.

On the other hand, keep to do same thing is avoid your charenge. When you try something that you don't like or new, it makes you unconfortable. When you face things that you don't understand well. It must be scared and unconfortable and then you have two choices. Charenge or escape. You don't need to always choose charenge, but you have to ask yourself, is escape good for you?

You need to have confortable time or things like hobbies. It must be good for you. But sometime you have to try to put yourself in unconfortable. It makes you improve and it brings knowledge.

Here is the examiner's comment:

This response does address the requirements of the question. There are relevant main ideas and an opinion in the concluding paragraph. However, the response is quite repetitive [*keep to do same thing*] and cohesion is faulty.

Vocabulary is generally adequate for the task, but there is a limited range with repeated errors in spelling [*unconfortable* / uncomfortable | *charenge* / challenge]. There are some attempts at complex sentence structures [*You don't need to always choose ... but*]; otherwise, sentences are short, indicating a lack of complexity. The level of error is significant in this response, including continuous structures [*keep to do* / keep doing | *you already used to do it* / you are already used to doing it].

This response is below the minimum word count for Task 2. The overall score could be improved if spelling and word choice were more accurate and if there was a wider variety in sentence structures.

TEST 3, WRITING TASK 1

This is an answer written by a candidate who achieved a **Band 7.0** score.

Dear Sir or Madam,

I am writing you in response to the article 'the book the influenced me most' printed in the last issue of your magazine, as it was stated there that you would be waiting for readers' contributions. Having noticed this, I couldn't have failed taking an opportunity to share my experience.

So, the book that literally turned my world upside down is called "Nina", by an italian author writing under the pen name of Moony Witcher. The book was about a girl who suddenly found out that her grandfather had not only been a great alchemist but had also kept saving the world from an evil mage. And it was her turn to take up his task and save all the children's dreams and fantasies from complete extinction.

I was twelve when I cracked this book open and I was completely lost in an interesting plot and a breathtaking philosophy concerning Good and Evil, Creation and Destruction, Everything and Nothing. This book had a great influence on me as a writer, it encouraged me to try writing fantasy stories and made me a person that I am now.

I would advise reading this book to everyone from age 8 to 16, as it is sure to be very beneficial for children's upbringing and to teach them some good things in a very interesting way.

Best regards,

Here is the examiner's comment:

> This response addresses all the requirements of the question. There is a good description of what the book was about and a clear idea of how it influenced the writer. To improve the score, more detail could be added to the final bullet point. The response is organised clearly into paragraphs and the cohesive devices make it easy to follow.
>
> Vocabulary is strong, there are some colloquial [*cracked ... open*] and higher-level items [*alchemist* | *fantasies* | *philosophy*]. There are also some good examples of complex grammatical structures but a few errors remain [*writing you* / writing to you | *a person* / the person].

TEST 3, WRITING TASK 2

This is an answer written by a candidate who achieved a **Band 6.0** score.

It is very common for many people to spend most of their lives living in the same city they were born. There are many reasons for that, but in my opinion there are more pros then cons to live in the same city.

Some advantages to live in the same city that you were born are you will be close to your family and that means you can have more support for them, for example, emotional or financial support or even advices. Another good point is you will see your nephews grow up and more important than that, you could help to take care of your parents when they get older. What is more you might have a lot of friends and if you live in the same city it is very easy to keep contact with them. Also, you will know the city, where it is good to have fun, where it is safe etc.

In the disadvantages side, if you live in the same city where were born you probably will lost the opportunity to meet people from another city. Also living alone far of your family you will grow up and be more responsible. What is more, you can have more jobs opportunities, because you can try to find a job in any city. Also you will have more adventures.

Even with some disadvantages, I think there are much more advantages to live in the same city that you were born.

Here is the examiner's comment:

> After the introduction, this response moves immediately into the advantages and disadvantages. This means there is no real reference to the first point, the 'reasons'. If the candidate had included the 'reasons', this response would have scored more highly.
>
> Paragraphing has been used to organise the ideas in this response. There is an introduction, a conclusion, one paragraph for advantages and another for disadvantages. Some effective cohesive devices are used, but overall, the response is a little repetitive [*Also*].
>
> Vocabulary is appropriate but the range is restricted, and sentences are generally short which limits the score for grammatical structures. Although the candidate is able to use a range of clauses [*if you live | because*], this is with some error.

TEST 4, WRITING TASK 1

This is an answer written by a candidate who achieved a **Band 5.0** score.

Dear Lisa,

I am so glad to help you to look for accommodation where is near my university. When I was at the university, I had been lived in an apartment for 4 years, which is offered to students or others from my school. It only takes 5 minutes on foot to the main gate of school, and it just takes 10 minutes on foot to the bus stop or train station. There has very convinent transport around my apartment. By the way, if you search apartment online, you should go to double check the information at reception. Because they might not update the information on time. So I advise you go to see the teacher who is in charge of accommodation at first. It will be saving more your time and energy.

What's more, when you are choosing accomdation, there are two suggestions for you:

First, please check the date that you are going to school. Is it any avilable accomadation for you at that date.

In addition, please make sure how long will you stay there. You are not able to get a refund even if you move out the accomadation earlier. So check how long is available you can stay.

At last, hopefully you can find a suitable accomodation soon and enjoy the life at university.

Friendly,

Here is the examiner's comment:

This is an attempt to provide advice on finding a place to live. All bullet points are touched on but not clearly presented, especially the third bullet point; there is no indication that this is a typical mistake students make. The format is appropriate for a letter despite the use of [*Friendly*] as a closing. The response presents the bullet points in the same order as the question. There is some good use of cohesive devices [*which* | *who*], but most are quite basic [*Because* | *So* | *In addition*] and faulty cohesion results in some repetition [*on foot* | *accommodation*].

The range of vocabulary is just adequate for the task but there are errors in spelling, even with the same word [*accomdation* | *accomadation* | *accomodation*]. There are some attempts at complex sentence structures [*even if*], but there are frequent errors in the use of articles and tenses [*had been lived* | *It will be saving more your time*], including the use of present tenses to talk about where they 'studied' in the past. These errors do cause some difficulty for the reader.

The Band Score could be improved if spelling and word choice were more accurate and if there was more accuracy in sentence structures.

TEST 4, WRITING TASK 2

This is an answer written by a candidate who achieved a **Band 7.0** score.

I personally agree with those who claim that the present days are the best period in the history of mankind to be living.

Breakthroughs in science and advancements in technology have dramatically improved our standards of living, at least in the Western world, making life actually worth living. Advances in medical treatments and the invention of new drugs all have allowed us to live long and healthy lives. We no longer face the problems of food and water scarcity, thanks to new agricultural techniques that allow farmers to produce larger quantities of food. Everyone, no matter its race and religion, can receive a proper education and make a decent living out of a good job. We should not also undervalue things such as the freedom of speech, which has not always been guaranteed in the past.

However, if I had the chance to choose an other time in our history to live in, I would opt for ancient Rome. I think it would be interesting to try living in a society whose beliefs and values significantly differs from our. In today's world, the most valuable personal "qualities" are selfishness and greed. We tend to put ourselves before other, whereas, in my opinion, things were different for the ancient civilizations, for wich the society as a whole came first.

In the end, I think we could learn some very interesting lessons from our past, without having to sacrifice all our the efforts made to get where we are today.

Here is the examiner's comment:

> This is a well-developed response which presents a range of evidence to justify the opinion expressed, including improvements in science, technology, medical treatments, agriculture, education, employment opportunities and freedom of speech. There is also a clear rationale for the 'other' time in history that would be interesting to live in.

> Ideas are arranged logically with one paragraph exploring each part of the question. However, we cannot say that paragraphing is used appropriately.

> The first and last paragraphs have only one sentence, and it is not clear if the final sentence is a new paragraph. The overall score of this response would be improved with an appropriate introductory and concluding paragraph. Other aspects of cohesion are good [*those who claim that* | *whose beliefs* | *to get where we are today*] with some slips [*its race* / their race | *our* / ours].

> The use of vocabulary is precise [*Breakthroughs in science and advancements in technology* | *making life … worth living* | *freedom of speech* | *ancient civilizations*] despite a few slips [*an other* / another | *wich* / which] and the range of grammatical structures is wide with frequent examples of error-free complex sentences. There are a few slips, e.g., third-person agreement [*differs* / differ] and plural ending [*before other* / before others], but overall there is good control.

Sample answer sheets

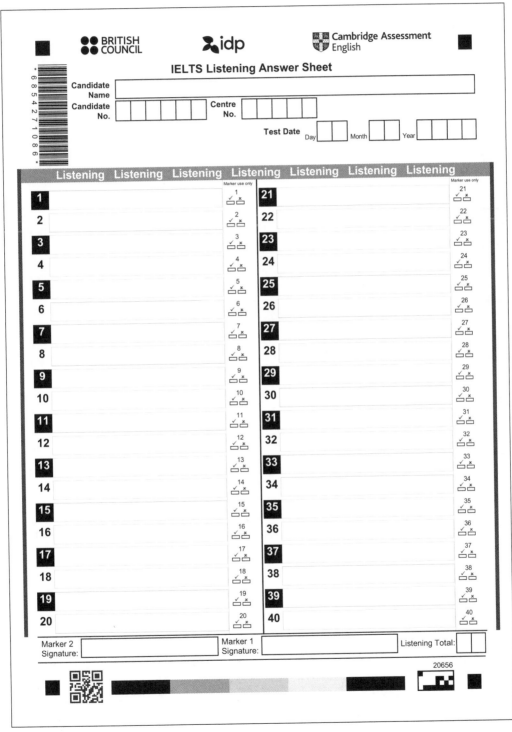

BRITISH COUNCIL

idp

Cambridge Assessment English

IELTS Listening Answer Sheet

Candidate Name

Candidate No.

Centre No.

Test Date   Day   Month   Year

Listening Listening Listening Listening Listening Listening Listening

1		21	
2		22	
3		23	
4		24	
5		25	
6		26	
7		27	
8		28	
9		29	
10		30	
11		31	
12		32	
13		33	
14		34	
15		35	
16		36	
17		37	
18		38	
19		39	
20		40	

Marker use only

Marker 2 Signature:

Marker 1 Signature:

Listening Total:

20656

© Cambridge Assessment 2021   Photocopiable

139

BRITISH COUNCIL **idp** **Cambridge Assessment English**

IELTS Reading Answer Sheet

Candidate Name

Candidate No.

Centre No.

Test Module ☐ Academic ☐ General Training

Test Date Day Month Year

Reading Reading Reading Reading Reading Reading Reading

#	Answer	Marker use only
1		1 ✓ ✗
2		2 ✓ ✗
3		3 ✓ ✗
4		4 ✓ ✗
5		5 ✓ ✗
6		6 ✓ ✗
7		7 ✓ ✗
8		8 ✓ ✗
9		9 ✓ ✗
10		10 ✓ ✗
11		11 ✓ ✗
12		12 ✓ ✗
13		13 ✓ ✗
14		14 ✓ ✗
15		15 ✓ ✗
16		16 ✓ ✗
17		17 ✓ ✗
18		18 ✓ ✗
19		19 ✓ ✗
20		20 ✓ ✗

#	Answer	Marker use only
21		21 ✓ ✗
22		22 ✓ ✗
23		23 ✓ ✗
24		24 ✓ ✗
25		25 ✓ ✗
26		26 ✓ ✗
27		27 ✓ ✗
28		28 ✓ ✗
29		29 ✓ ✗
30		30 ✓ ✗
31		31 ✓ ✗
32		32 ✓ ✗
33		33 ✓ ✗
34		34 ✓ ✗
35		35 ✓ ✗
36		36 ✓ ✗
37		37 ✓ ✗
38		38 ✓ ✗
39		39 ✓ ✗
40		40 ✓ ✗

Marker 2 Signature:

Marker 1 Signature:

Reading Total:

61788

BRITISH COUNCIL

idp

Cambridge Assessment English

IELTS Writing Answer Sheet - TASK 1

Candidate Name

Candidate No.

Centre No.

Test Module   ☐ Academic   ☐ General Training

Test Date   Day   Month   Year

If you need more space to write your answer, use an additional sheet and write in the space provided to indicate how many sheets you are using: Sheet   of

Writing   Task 1   Writing   Task 1   Writing   Task 1   Writing   Task 1

Do not write below this line

Do not write in this area. Please continue your answer on the other side of this sheet.

23505

BRITISH COUNCIL

idp

Cambridge Assessment English

IELTS Writing Answer Sheet - TASK 2

Candidate Name	

Candidate No.   Centre No.

Test Module   ☐ Academic   ☐ General Training   **Test Date**   Day   Month   Year

If you need more space to write your answer, use an additional sheet and write in the space provided to indicate how many sheets you are using: Sheet   of

Writing Task 2   Writing Task 2   Writing Task 2   Writing Task 2

Do not write below this line

Do not write in this area. Please continue your answer on the other side of this sheet.

39507

© Cambridge Assessment 2021   Photocopiable

Acknowledgements

The authors and publishers acknowledge the following sources of copyright material and are grateful for the permissions granted. While every effort has been made, it has not always been possible to identify the sources of all the material used, or to trace all copyright holders. If any omissions are brought to our notice, we will be happy to include the appropriate acknowledgements on reprinting and in the next update to the digital edition, as applicable.

Key: L = Listening, R = Reading

Text
L1: Ryan Holiday for the adapted text from 'Stoicism: Practical Philosophy You Can Actually Use' by Ryan Holiday. Copyright © Ryan Holiday. Reproduced with kind permission; **R1:** Health & Safety Authority for the adapted text from, 'Reducing the Risk of Back Injuries on the Farm'. Courtesy of Health & Safety Authority; High Speed Training Ltd. for the adapted text from 'What Defines Good Customer Service in Retail?' by Jordan Bradley, 03.12.2015, www.highspeedtraining.co.uk. Copyright © High Speed Training Ltd. Reproduced with kind permission; The Financial Times Limited for the adapted text from 'Why plastic is no longer fantastic', by Gillian Tett, Opinion, FT.COM, 17.11.2017. Copyright © The Financial Times Limited. Reproduced with permission; **R2:** Johanna Leggatt for the adapted text from 'How to choose your builder: Do your research before signing up' by Johanna Leggatt, Home, 31.10.2015. Copyright © Johanna Leggatt. Reproduced with permission; Visit Isle of Wight Ltd. for the adapted text from 'the Isle of Wight: Pure Wight Adrenaline (2017) Funded by the Isle of Wight Business Improvement District'. Copyright © Visit Isle of Wight Ltd. Reproduced with kind permission; Ancient History Encyclopedia for the adapted text from 'Jobs in ancient Egypt' by Joshua J. Mark. 24.05.2017. Copyright © Ancient History Encyclopedia. Reproduced with permission; **R3:** Seasons For Coffee Ltd. for the adapted text from '7 Qualities That Make An Effective Barista', 09.07.2016. Copyright © Seasons For Coffee Ltd. Reproduced with kind permission; Seeds for Change for the adapted text from 'Organising Successful Meetings', www. seedsforchange.org.uk/meeting. Copyright © Seeds for Change. Reproduced with kind permission; University of Cambridge for the adapted text from 'Research Horizons', Issue 34, October 2017. Copyright © University of Cambridge. Reproduced with kind permission; **R4:** Craft Courses Ltd for the adapted text from 'Beekeeping for Beginners Workshop'. Copyright © Craft Courses Ltd. Reproduced with kind permission; The Guardian for the adapted text from 'Should you pay someone to write your CV?' by Clare Whitmell, *The Guardian*, 09.04.2010. Copyright © 2020 Guardian News & Media Ltd. Reproduced with permission; Hired, Inc. for the adapted text from 'First Day at New Job! 7 Things to Do on Your First Day' by Alyssa Seidman. 08.04.2016. Copyright © Hired, Inc. Reproduced with kind permission; Immediate Media Company Ltd. for the adapted text from '1921: the year when football banned women', *History Extra*, December 2017. Copyright © Immediate Media Company Ltd. Reproduced with permission.

Illustration
Illustrations commissioned by Cambridge Assessment

Audio
Audio production by dsound recording studios

Typesetting
Typeset by QBS Learning

URLs
The publisher has used its best endeavours to ensure that the URLs for external websites referred to in this book are correct and active at the time of going to press. However, the publisher has no responsibility for the websites and can make no guarantee that a site will remain live or that the content is or will remain appropriate

Practice Makes Perfect

By teachers for teachers

Get more out of Authentic Practice Tests

Lesson Plans

Teacher Tips

Extra Support

- Get Tips and Tricks to use in your classroom
- Download practice test Lesson Plans
- Explore the extra support, training and technology available for your exam

Find out more at
practicemakesperfect.cambridge.org